101 Relationship Myths

How to Stop Them from Sabotaging Your Happiness

Also by Tim Ray

Starbrow: A Spiritual Adventure
Starwarrior: A Spiritual Thriller
The Awakening Human Being: A Guide to the Power of Mind
(by Barbara Berger with Tim Ray)

101 Relationship Myths

How to Stop Them from Sabotaging Your Happiness

Tim Ray

FINDHORN PRESS

Published in 2012 by Findhorn Press, Scotland

ISBN 978-1-84409-584-1

Edited by Barbara Berger
Front cover design, including photograph by Richard Crookes
Back cover photograph by Søren Solkær Starbird
Interior design by Damian Keenan
Printed and bound in the EU

1 2 3 4 5 6 7 8 9 17 16 15 14 13 12

Published by

Findhorn Press

117-121 High Street,

Forres IV36 1AB,

Scotland, UK

t +44 (0)1309 690582

f +44 (0)131 777 2711

e info@findhornpress.com

www.findhornpress.com

Heartfelt Thanks To

Barbara — You have enriched my life.

Byron Katie — For The Work.

Jens, Signe, Henrik and my many friends on levlykkeligt.dk
 — For stimulating debate on relationship myths.

My readers, and everyone who has been to my lectures,
workshops and private sessions — thanks for everything
you've taught me.

Pernille — "All I really want to do is,
baby, be friends with you."

And last, but not least: My amazing ex-girlfriends —
I'm so grateful.

Contents

Contents

Prologue:
Are relationships the work
of the Devil?

Once upon a time many thousands of years ago, the Devil himself was sitting in his boiling hot corporate headquarters in Hell, looking at his mission statement, which was hanging on the wall in big flaming red letters at the other end of his office. It read:

"To make as many people as possible
as unhappy as possible
for as long as possible."

The Devil was actually a bit depressed because he felt that it really wasn't going so well for the Devil & Co,'s mission at the moment. Despite his persistent efforts, people all around the world were generally very happy and satisfied. People were just loafing around loving themselves and each other and feeling really quite good about everything.

So the Devil knew he had to do something drastic if he was going to avoid being transferred, degraded—or worse—fired. He would have to come up with something that would really kick ass and make people feel dreadfully unhappy and desperate.

And that was when he got the most brilliant idea! An idea that would—without a shadow of a doubt—really make his mission and vision of making as many people as possible as unhappy as possible for as long as possible—a reality. And the idea was...

RELATIONSHIPS!

Yes! Of course, that was it! The Devil could already see it. *Relationships*—the direct route to Hell! One big lie—or a pack of lies—that were so huge and convincing that they would make people desperately unhappy right from childhood...

The Devil started frantically writing his plan down:

The Devil's Lie No. 1 about Relationships:
The love that I seek is outside me.

Like whoa! This is brilliant, just brilliant, thought the Devil, as he hopped up and down enthusiastically on his flaming red throne. If I can just get enough people to believe that the love they seek is outside themselves... it will be truly awesome. So awesome that the Devil & Co. will probably end up being listed on the New York Stock Exchange!

Brilliant. Now that the basic concept was in place, it was time to add a little more pain... hee, hee, hee.

The Devil's Lie No. 2 about Relationships:
The love that I seek is dependent on another person.

Like whoa again! This is good, really, really good thought the Devil, surprised by his own ingenuity. I'm really something... Yes, I really am. Amazing... And here's another one...!

The Devil's Lie No. 3 about Relationships:
I can only experience the love that I seek with one special person.

Even more brilliant! Sometimes I just surprise myself. He could already see the Devil & Co.'s worldwide advertising campaign supported by Internet banners in every language proclaiming things like "The One and Only", "Soul Mates", "The Love of Your Life" ... Brilliant, brilliant. This is just brilliant. The Devil could already feel the confusion, the overwhelming longing, the terrible misery and loneliness that people would feel, all the way down to his fifteen big toes. Millions and millions of people all around the world who would actually believe that they could only experience the love they seek with one special person — without ever quite knowing who this one special person was!

And if one was actually lucky enough to find this person, there was no guarantee that this person would return the love. No guarantee that he or she wasn't already in another relationship. Yes it was brilliant! Just brilliant!

If the Devil could get people to believe this, it would truly be the end of all that nauseating, touchy-feely lovey-dovey stuff that was flourishing on earth at the moment. It would be the end of all those happy people who just went around loving everything and everyone…

And last but not least…

The Devil's Lie No. 4 about Relationships:
It's only true love if the relationship lasts forever.

Yes! Now that's good—that's got to hurt! With this lie, the Devil could be sure that people would stay unhappy no matter what. If they weren't in a relationship, they'd be unhappy because they'd believe that the love that they seek was outside themselves and dependent on another person. If they were in a relationship where the partners drifted apart, well this devilish lie—(that it's only true love if the relationship lasts forever)—would keep them in the relationship no matter what they really felt. And the few who actually would be brave enough to separate would always look back at the relationship and feel it was one big failure.

Hmm….The Devil was aware that this last lie was rather far out and that it would be pretty difficult to get people to believe it. So he figured he'd add a little extra lie to back this one up. He decided he'd spread the word that it was God Himself—the Top Dog—who proclaimed this lie to be the God's Honest Truth. The Devil would make sure that all religions in the world taught that a relationship was only genuine and real if the partners took a solemn oath that they would love each other and stay together forever—no matter what!

Ha ha ha. Am I brilliant or what? The Devil just couldn't stop slapping his thighs with pure devilish joy.

Okay—so far so good. Now it was time for action—and not just a little action. No, no, no. The Devil knew that if he was going to sell such a colossal pack of lies to humanity, he'd really have to roll out the most massive brainwashing campaign the world had ever seen. So he called in all his top executives and his sales and marketing people and his branding department and they all worked day and night developing a campaign that would make even the most incredible lies like racism, nationalism, sexism, ageism and materialism fade in comparison. The Devil's campaign of lies would be a mega-giga-super-duper advertising campaign about "The One and Only" made up of a million trillion pop songs and music videos and TV series and movies and women's magazine articles and books and novels, backed by the fashion and cosmetic industries—all broadcasting non-stop day and night the Devil's pack of lies about relationships….

Now I wonder how the Devil's brilliant plan turned out…

Introduction:
A little about this book

One of the biggest heartbreaks in my life is probably the main reason why you are sitting with this book in your hand today.

I'd been with a woman for several years and we'd had some really good years together. Then suddenly things turned sour. No matter what we did, we had problems — problems communicating, problems being honest with each other, and problems showing and sharing our love. Finally the whole thing turned into one big non-stop drama with all the usual arguments and tears. Every day brought another new and painful episode. I felt as if my heart was being torn apart. Every thought, every word was like a knife in the gaping wound that had once been my heart. I was so unhappy and depressed, I couldn't think straight. In the end, I seriously considered jumping off the nearest bridge and drowning myself in the ice cold sea. Then, I thought, it would at least be over!

Yet, the interesting thing about crisis is that it often leads to something new and better. In this case, all the pain I felt in those days became the start of a fantastic journey of discovery that transformed my life. As it turned out, the pain motivated me to try to find out what it was all about. To try to understand how a relationship that was once so happy and loving could suddenly become so unhappy and problematic. Was it just me? Was there something wrong with me? Was I suffering from some kind of psychological defect or trauma that made me have so many problems in my relationship? Or was great pain just a part of great love, as the poets say?

And if it was me, well then what about my girlfriend? And what about the girlfriends I had before her? And what about all their partners and ex-partners? And what about all the other people in the world who have problems with their relationships? Because it was obvious I wasn't the only one who had relationship problems!

So I decided to dedicate myself— no matter what the cost—to finding some answers. After a relatively short time, it was as if suddenly a light went on in my inner darkness and I began to see that (hallelujah!) there was nothing wrong with me or with anyone else. I realized that the reason I'd been so un-happy in my last relationship and in some of my previous relationships was that I wasn't aware of the fact that I was innocently believing a lot of thoughts, ideas and stories about relationships that simply didn't have anything to do with real-ity! It was amazing! Suddenly, it was starting to make sense. All these thoughts and ideas I so innocently believed in — well they are what I today call the *101 relationship myths.*

And so this book was born! Born out of my discovery and my investigation of these innocent thoughts, these innocent relationship myths that sabotage our happiness!

Four simple observations

My exploration of our collective myths about relationships is based on four simple observations about this thing we call life. Here are my four observations:

OBSERVATION NO. 1:
There is a difference between reality and your thinking
The first observation is that reality — what is happening right now — is one thing, while our thoughts (yours and mine) are often something completely different.

Let's take a simple example. Let's say your partner didn't call you last night. (You are in a relationship with this person but you don't live together.) Your partner said that he (or she) would call you last night, but didn't. That is reality. That's what happened. But you can have a wide variety of thoughts about what happened — and your thoughts may be something very different from reality. Here's what I mean. Perhaps you are thinking, "My boyfriend *should* have called last night" or "Isn't he selfish?" or "Isn't he inconsiderate?" or maybe you are even thinking, "He's probably with someone else." All of these thoughts may or may not have anything to do with reality. Once you have one of these thoughts, they probably give birth to other thoughts such as, "He doesn't love me anymore," or "I'm not good enough," or "There must be something wrong with me". And then these thoughts may give rise to even more thoughts and stories which are moving you further and further from reality. Because what was the reality? What do you actually know for sure? What are the facts here? Well, the only thing you know for sure is that your partner didn't call last night. But why he didn't call — well that's some-thing you don't know at the moment. Maybe he forgot to call. Maybe he fell asleep. Or maybe his father had a heart attack and he ended up sitting with him in the hospital all night. Or maybe… As you can see, there could be a million reasons why your partner didn't call. Right now, all you know is that your partner didn't call as promised. That's reality.

OBSERVATION NO. 2:
There is a cause and effect relationship between your thinking and your experience. Thought is cause, experience is effect.
The next observation is that every time you think a thought and believe it, you experience the effect of believing in that thought. Every time you believe a thought, it starts a chain of reactions in your life. When you believe a thought, it affects your feelings, your physical body, the way you talk, your behavior and your relationships with other people. Because thought (in other words, what you really believe in) is cause and your experience is the effect of what you believe in. This holds true whether or not the thought has anything to do with reality.

So, what happens when your partner didn't call last night and you believe thoughts such as, "He *should* have called," "He's only thinking of himself," "He doesn't love me anymore"? How does this affect you when you believe thoughts like this? Maybe you feel angry, hurt or unhappy. Maybe you start to tense up physically and your body begins to shut down. Maybe you get a headache or a stomachache. Maybe you have difficulty concentrating on what you're doing at work because you can't stop thinking about your partner. Maybe next time you're with your partner, you are cold and withdrawn and maybe you even snap his or her head off. And so on. All because of the thoughts you're having, thoughts which you're not even sure have anything to do with reality.

OBSERVATION NO. 3:
When your thoughts are out of harmony with reality, you experience discomfort, stress and unhappiness.
With a clear understanding of the first two observations, we can also now better understand why we often experience discomfort, stress and unhappiness in our lives and in our relationships. We do this because our thinking is out of harmony with reality. Every time you resist reality, every time you believe that reality (for example your partner) "should" be different from the way it is right now—you feel bad. In other words, you experience some degree of stress and discomfort.

Because reality is what it is. Whatever happens has already happened. Either your partner called you last night or he didn't. And if the reality is he didn't call, well, then there's nothing you can do about it. You can beg and pray and shout and scream but it won't change the fact that your partner didn't call you last night. (How you react to the fact that your partner didn't call you last night is another thing. But the fact is, he didn't call and nothing can change that.)

Reality is always stable. It is what it is. Every time we don't see reality and instead believe our stories and let ourselves be run by stories which don't have anything to do with reality, it feels uncomfortable. In fact, the discomfort we feel is the way life lets us know that our thinking is out of harmony with reality.

OBSERVATION NO. 4:
You can end your discomfort, stress and unhappiness (and experience more happiness and peace) by bringing your thinking into harmony with reality.
When we clearly understand why we experience discomfort and unhappiness in our lives, we can also better see how we can end our discomfort and unhappiness and experience more happiness and peace. We can do this by bringing our thinking into harmony with reality. The same mental process that made you unhappy you can now consciously use to end your discomfort and unhappiness. As a result, you will experience more clarity, happiness and peace in your life and in your relationship.

How would you do this in the example of the partner who didn't call last night? Well, it's really very simple. You simply stick to reality. You stick to what is right now, and that is: *my partner didn't call me last night.* Period. Full stop. That's all you know.

So, how do you deal with this reality? Well, there are many possibilities. If you are wondering if your partner is OK, well, you could call and ask. If you don't feel like doing that, well, maybe you just enjoy having a nice quiet evening by yourself — or maybe you call a friend and hang out with her instead. The next time you talk to your partner, you can ask why he or she didn't call last night as promised. So there are many options — and they are all options that are based on reality — instead of on assumptions about things you don't know for sure.

As you start to become more aware of the difference between reality and your thinking, and of the cause and effect relationship between your thinking and your experience, you will also begin to see how this mechanism is working in all areas of your life. In other words, you will see how your thinking affects your experience at work, your experience of your own body and your experiences with other people as well.

Relationship myths

Your thoughts, beliefs and stories about relationships (and about men, women, sex, falling in love, attraction, love, commitment, parents, children and everything else that is associated with relationships) determine — for better or for worse — your experience of your relationship. Every time your thoughts about relationships or your partner are out of harmony with reality, every time your actions are based on a story or expectation that is out of harmony with reality, you will experience some degree of discomfort in your relationship. This discomfort can swing from mild irritation to deep unhappiness and despair — which is exactly what I found out so many years ago when I was about to jump off that bridge. I found out that my confusion and pain (and other people's confusion and pain) when it comes to relationships arises when we believe thoughts and stories about relationships that don't have anything to do with reality.

I also found out that these thoughts and stories about relationships aren't personal. By that, I mean they're not particularly yours or mine. Rather, these stories are collective and universal. In other words, everyone has them, which is why I call them "myths". Most people believe in these myths to a greater or lesser degree. Why is this so? Because we learned these myths from our parents (who learned them from their parents) and in school and from our surroundings. So, these stories have been passed down from generation to generation. Since most people don't question these myths, they continue to run our lives and our relationships to this very day.

The good news is that we can question these relationship myths! I found out that we can look at them and ask ourselves whether or not they have anything to do with reality. By doing this, we can end our unhappiness and experience more happiness and true love — not just in our relationships with our partners, but in all our relationships.

One of the interesting extra benefits of working with your thoughts about relationships is that you discover you have pretty much the same thoughts about all the other people in your life as you have about your partner. So, if you're not good at setting limits and saying no to your partner as a result of your beliefs, then you're probably also not good at setting limits and saying no to other members of your family and to your friends and colleagues. If this is the case, then as you become more conscious of these beliefs and learn to set limits and say no to your partner in a firm, loving manner, this will automatically help you set limits and say no in a good way in all your other relationships. If you have unrealistic expectations of your partner which sometimes make you feel disappointed, angry or hurt, then you probably also have unrealistic expectations of the other people in your life (such as to your mother or sister or boss!). Again, this means if you learn to see your partner more realistically, you will probably also start seeing the other people in your life more realistically too. So, you discover that the work you do in one area of your life has a positive influence on other areas of your life as well.

How this book is designed

When writing this book, I tried to:

1. Identify some of our most basic collective relationship myths
2. Investigate how much (or how little) these myths have to do with reality
3. Describe some of the unhappy consequences that arise when we believe in these myths and let them run our lives and our relationships
4. Explore how our lives and our relationships could be if we didn't believe in these myths anymore

In Part One of the book, I look closely at typical relationship situations and at some of the myths which arise in these situations. Myths such as: "If you love me, you'll do what I want," "If I try hard enough, my partner will sooner or later change," "A relationship can only work if you compromise," or "Strong sexual attraction means we're a good match." Then in each chapter, I investigate how much the given myth has to do with reality. I try to describe some of the often absurd and unhappy consequences that believing these myths can have for us. Next, I explore, or invite you to explore, how your relationship with your partner would be if you were living more in harmony with reality.

In Part Two of the book, it's your turn. Here, I present some simple myth-busting techniques that you can use here and now to identify and investigate relationship myths and experience more clarity, joy and love in your relationship.

At the end of the book, there is a short overview of the different techniques and exercises to help you quickly get an idea of which techniques are good for the different situations and challenges you may be facing in your relationship.

How to get the most out of this book

You can either read the book from start to finish — or you can simply turn to any chapter in Part One that attracts your attention and just read and work with that specific issue.

Of course you'll benefit most from this book if you investigate the myths yourself instead of just reading my conclusions. This is especially true when it comes to the myths that you believe in or which are causing problems in your life and your relationship.

To make it easy for you, at the end of each chapter I've listed the main myth or myths discussed in the chapter. So if you read a chapter and want to investigate the myth yourself, all you need to do is write down the myth and then use the simple mythbusting technique I describe in Part Two of the book to examine it.

The next step is to start incorporating your new insights into your daily life—and this of course requires practice! But the results are definitely well worth the effort.

Good reading and happy mythbusting!

PART ONE

101 Relationship Myths

MYTH *[mith]: a traditional or legendary story, with or without a determinable basis of fact; an unproved collective belief that is accepted uncritically.*

Women's magazines — the biggest champions of relationship myths!

Reading about relationships in women's magazines can either make you laugh or cry, depending on how you look at it. Why? Because so many of these articles are based on our common relationship myths that the articles really have very little if anything to do with reality. Just take a look at the supposedly serious article below from the women's magazine *Woman*. It's about having a relationship with someone who's either a lot older or a lot younger than you are. I think you will enjoy it. Especially when you read my comments, which are inserted in the text in italics. What I've done is point out every time there's something in the article that is based on a relationship myth.

Here's the article:

Grave robber or cradle robber?
Good advice if you're together with someone a lot older or younger
BY SIGNE LØNHOLDT

Live in the present, but think about the future

Many couples with a big age difference between the partners live in the present and don't consider how things will be in the future. [*Is this true? I have yet to meet a person who only lives in the now and doesn't think about how things are going to be in the future!*] Perhaps it's frightening to think 10 years ahead. One of the partners in the relationship will be old while the other will still be relatively young. On the other hand, the age difference means less as you become older. A 20-year-old woman and a 35-year-old man will probably have less in common than a 50-year-old woman and a 65-year-old man. [*Is this true?*]

This is because one's personality really changes a lot when you're in your 20s and 30s. [*Is this true? The psychological studies I've read show that the thoughts and basic beliefs that make up a person's personality are formed in one's childhood and don't change very much after that.*] So you could wake up one morning and find that you've outgrown the person you loved so much. That is why it's especially important for couples with a big age difference to talk to each other about the changes they are experiencing all the time. [*Why is it more important than for a couple where the age difference isn't so big? Is it true that people in one age group are different from people in another age group?*]

People in their 30s, 40s and 50s are much more active and in much better shape than people their age just 10 years ago, so a few years plus or minus don't really matter psychologically [*Is it true?*]. In today's world, a big age difference between the partners may not mean so much. [*Is it true? Then why is she writing an article about relationships with big age differences?*] Getting a relationship to work may be more important. The most important thing is that the two people have something in common because if you want to go to town and party and he wants to play golf you will probably drift apart as time goes by. [*Is this true? Can't you have a good relationship even if you have different interests? Can you only have a good relationship if you do everything or almost everything together? And is there anything wrong with drifting apart as time goes by? Is a relationship only a success if it lasts a long time or until death do us part? Is a long, unhappy relationship better than a short, happy one?*] Of course it is important for each party to have their own interests [*Is it true?*]. It's important that you both have your own friends your own age or with the same interests. [*Is it true? Why is it important to have friends your own age? Isn't it just as good to have a friend who's not the same age as you? What does age have to do with friendship—or with anything for that matter? Also is it true that people of different ages are different?*]. But make sure you have something in common—if nothing else then at least your relationship.

Not too long ago the media revealed that the not-so-young fashion model Helena Christensen had her claws in 10-years-younger Josh Hartnett. [*Is that true? Did she contact him or did he contact her? Did she chase him or did he chase her?*]. Plus, they're not the only couple in Hollywood with a big age difference. In fact, it's almost become a sport to find a boyfriend/girlfriend who is either a lot older or a lot younger than oneself. *[Is it true?]* Maybe you are one of the people who's following the trend. *[Is it true? And if you are in a relationship where there's a big age difference, is it because you are following a trend?]* Here are a few tips for women who like Sugar Daddies or Boy Toys.

If there is more than five years age difference between you and your partner, you can place yourself in the category "Partners with a big age difference".

Maybe you think that men your own age are too immature and are still just fooling around, so you'd rather have a more experienced and serious man. Or maybe you find men your own age way too serious and too focused on their careers — they forget to play and be impulsive so you would rather have a man who is much younger and freer. *[Older men are more down to earth and serious about their careers while younger men are more free and impulsive — is that true?]*

But be sure what your motives are before you start the relationship. *[How do you do that? How can you become more conscious of what your motives are — and if this is so important, why doesn't she say anything about this in this article?]* Is it because you want to be a mother for him or is it because he is the father figure you always longed for? Is he a young trophy or a stable economic support? If you choose him for the wrong reasons *[Is it "wrong" to choose a partner because you're attracted to his/her physical appearance or his/her money? What then are the "right" reasons?]*, the relationship will be difficult because things can suddenly change — and he won't need a mother anymore or the money can disappear.

The rest of the family

The reaction of your friends and family may not be so positive the first time you tell them that your new partner is 10 years younger or older than you are. If he is older, they might not understand what you see in him — and if he is younger, they will be betting that he will leave you when you get older. But remember this is because they want the best for you, so listen to what they say. *[Why? Is it true that what your friends and family say is true? Have your friends and family learned to see the difference between reality and their thoughts?*

Do they know what's best for you?]. Maybe they will say something wise you can use. If they don't, well just let whatever they say go in one ear and out the other and be happy that you've found the man in your life.

In any case, it's important to have friends so even if they don't take the news so positively at first, try to make them understand [*I can make my friends understand how I feel—is that true?*] that you and your new partner really are good for each other despite the age difference. It can in fact be difficult for you and your new love to find friends who are in the same boat as you and it's always nice to have someone you can talk to about life and love, so why not keep your old friends?

———

Marvelous, right? High-level entertainment, right?

The statements above that I questioned are only a few examples of the many things in this article about love, happiness, men, women and age that one could question.

So I ask you, if this is where women today get their information about relationships, is it any wonder that so many feel confused and frustrated when it comes to relationships (whether they're single, just having a fling, married or divorced)? And if their partners also buy into these myths, is it any wonder that so many people are so confused when it comes to love?

Stay away from women in their 30s!

Why? Because women in their 30s are really bad news! Why do I say that? Because when a woman is in her 30s, she believes that the good life, the perfect life, the sweet life is just around the corner if she just works hard enough and is good enough. She believes utterly and completely that as a result of all her dedicated efforts, she will soon have this perfect life (the one the glossy women's magazines are shoving down our throats and telling us is the royal road to eternal happiness). You know the life with the perfect man, the perfect relationship, the perfect kids, the perfect family, the great sex life, the perfect, sexy body, the perfect high-powered career, the perfect, beautiful home with the perfect designer furniture... not to mention the perfect quality weekends, the picture-perfect holidays! Yes, that's it... her dream... the superb lifestyle with more and more and more quality.

It's simply so exhausting to be around a woman in her 30s that it makes me sick to my stomach (and believe me, I've had quite a few girlfriends in their 30s). So now every time I meet a woman in her 30s, I look for the nearest exit — because I know having a relationship with a woman in her 30s means big-time stress!

Now I stick to women in their 20s or 40s or older, because even if women in their 20s still believe the dream that if you just work hard enough, one day you will achieve all these things and be happy — at least most women in their 20s have the attitude "But not just yet. I still want a few years of fun before I sign up for the female version of the Foreign Legion-Navy Seals-Iron Woman-Miss Sex and the City meets House & Garden syndrome." (Though it's true, I've also met a few unfortunate women in their late 20s who are already infected with this seriously life-threatening form of insanity).

And then there are women over 40 — thank God! They are usually even more fun than women in their 20s because women over 40 as a rule no longer have such illusions. Women in their 40s or older have worked themselves to the bone day and night to live up to the dream that says if they just manage to achieve this or that they'll be happy—and now they're over 40 and guess what—it didn't happen. The bubble burst! Either they didn't achieve all the things they thought would make them happy—the man, children, family, job, career, beautiful home, designer furniture, friends, picture-perfect holidays and so forth (and are now simply worn out, burnt out and unhappy from working so hard for so many years). Or they did achieve all the things they believed were necessary to be happy—and they're still not happy. Now they realize the game's over, the race is run and that despite all their dedicated efforts they're just not getting any younger or more beautiful or healthier or stronger. The reality is their kids just keep on growing and their husbands and boyfriends aren't getting any smarter, and getting the latest, hottest new possessions—whatever they are—just don't seem to make anything better anymore. Just think… all those years, all that hard work — and now it's almost game over. So they begin to realize that if they don't start living life now and start having some fun now, they're never going to really live and have fun. So guess what! Hallelujah… women in their 40s begin to drop the cherished female version of the Foreign Legion-Navy Seals-Iron Woman-Miss Sex and the City meets House & Garden syndrome and actually start focusing a little more on relaxing, breathing and enjoying life. Which of course is why it's so much more fun to be with women who are over 40! Unless of course they're still stubbornly hanging on to the glossy magazine dreams (and I have to admit I have met a few pitiful examples who were still fighting a losing battle to keep the old dream alive). But whenever I met a woman in her 40s who is still like this I think, why worry—sooner or later she'll hit that wall and go into meltdown mode.

So yes… this is why I say, stay far, far away from women in their 30s! And if you're a woman in your 30s—it might be a good idea to stop trying to live up to society's idea of what a woman in her 30s should be like—that is if you want to make it through your 30s with your sanity somewhat intact!

Stay away from women
in their 30s!

PART 2

After reading part one of this chapter, you might be thinking, Is this just one man venting his anger at his ex-girlfriends and women in their 30s? But hand on my heart, it's not. I just wanted to get your attention so we could take a serious look at something much deeper and more fundamental. Issues like:

- We live in a society where everyone (women and men) is constantly bombarded and brainwashed (from the moment we are born and for the rest of our lives) to accept the most insane beliefs about what it takes to be OK, good, live a happy life and be loved.

- The really stressful consequences of these insane beliefs often really become apparent when women are in their 30s.

Why is this so? Why does this happen? Why is it that the unfortunate consequences of our insane beliefs and sky-high collective expectations often become really apparent in women when they are in their 30s?

I believe there are many factors that contribute to the strange behavior of women in their 30s. Here are some of them:

When we're in our 30s, the collective
relationship myths really kick in

As I wrote in the introduction, we have been programmed from childhood to believe in the 101 relationships myth. But when I look back at my life and the lives of my contemporaries, I can see that these myths often first really begin to sabotage our happiness when we're in our 30s. Not that we didn't believe in these myths when we were younger, it's just that the unpleasant consequences of these beliefs don't really begin to manifest until we're in our 30s.

Why is this so?

One of the reasons is that we live in a society where it's socially acceptable NOT to live up to our sky-high expectations about relationships, marriage and family when you're in your 20s. When you're in your 20s, it's socially acceptable to enjoy life and live a little more in the present moment. Someone in their 20s is not expected to worry too much about the future even though there are some people in their 20s who are already worrying themselves sick about their future relationships and even their pension plan!

But when you're in your 30s, things are different. Then the whole relationship thing suddenly becomes serious business because now the clock is ticking. When you enter the 30s, there's no more time for just fooling around. Now it's time to think about the future! And so the 101 relationship myths really kick in — and begin to sabotage everyone's happiness.

There is, however, one very important detail that cranks up the stress for women — and that is …

Biology!
Men can have children long after 40 —
and women can't!

As many women in their 30s have indignantly said to me: "It's just so unfair that men can still have children when they're over 40 and we women can't. So that means when we're in our 30s, our biological clock is really ticking — and ticking loud! Since most of us want children, well when we're in our 30s it's now or never. So of course we can't go on wasting our time on men or relationships which won't end with children. We've got to be sure, we've got to have guarantees! We have to think about the future!"

This puts a lot more pressure on women in their 30s when it comes to relationships than on men. Men in their 30s just don't feel the same sense of urgency when it comes to having kids — instead they just feel it from their partners!

History!
Women are more identified with
relationship myths than men

Another reason why relationship myths hit women harder is history. When you look at things from the historical perspective, you discover that women have traditionally had much more of their identity bound up in relationships than men.

Up until recently, there were very few areas in life that were open to women. Men always had the freedom to make their mark via their jobs and careers and they could participate freely in politics, the world of art, or choose a religious pathway. Men have always had many options as well as the financial freedom and independence to express themselves in the world. But until recently this wasn't the case for women. Women were denied access to most of these areas and could not work, make money, vote, be politicians, etc. Historically, the only area where women could use their influence (and manifest their power) was in the area of family, relationships, and children. (Think about Jane Austen's scathing depictions of women's lives and circumstances in Merry Old England not so very long ago.)

With so little freedom, is it any wonder that family and relationships became so very important to women — to their lives and their identities?

So what does that mean today? Could it be that even today, despite the fact that women in the Western world (at least in principle) now have the freedom to participate in most areas of life on an equal footing with men that they are still unconsciously influenced by so many generations of limitation and traditional conditioning when it comes to a woman's role in society? Is this one of the reasons why women today are still so identified with relationships and family?

The Superwoman syndrome

So what happens when we combine all these factors — the collective relationship myths, women's biological nature, women's historical role in society — with the sky-high expectations women in our society today are being bombarded with from all sides? What happens when a woman tries to lives up to the superwoman scenario, which says she should be the perfect wife, the perfect mother, the perfect homemaker, the perfect hot, sexy lover, the perfect career woman while having the perfect designer home and being the perfect friend to her friends (and don't forget baking homemade cookies for her kids when they come home from kindergarten)? In short, what happens when a woman falls victim to what I call the female version of the Foreign Legion-Navy Seals-Iron Woman-Miss Sex and the City-meets-House & Garden syndrome?

All I can say is, Is it any wonder that so many women in their 30s have become ticking stress bombs and finally begin to crack?

Is there anyone (even superwoman) who can possibly live up to such constant, massive pressure and such sky-high expectations? Do you know anyone who can? If you do, if some poor woman actually succeeds in becoming this perfect woman for a while, how long will it last? How long until she burns out? How long will she be able to live up to such massive pressure? How long can anyone stand pressure like this? So sooner or later a crisis will come — be it physical or mental or both. Something just has to give. That's when people will shake their heads and say: Oh, poor woman, she's suffering from stress! Stress. Yeah, right!

After the crisis comes disillusionment

For many years now I have been giving lectures and workshops and doing private sessions with a focus on how we can live happier, more satisfying lives by bringing our thinking into harmony with reality. In the beginning I used to wonder why most of the people attending were women ages 35-45. I wondered where are people in their 20s or people in their 60s or older? And why are there so few men?

But now I am starting to understand because I've discovered that there's a connection between the massive pressure society places on women in their 30s and the fact that many women become interested in self-help and personal development when they reach their late 30s. In fact, 37 or 38 seem to be the years when many women experience some form of crisis. Suddenly they can't go on; they burn out.

Then what happens? What happens when you're in crisis and become disillusioned? What happens when you begin to realize that all the outer things you thought would make you happy can't really do it at all? And that in fact, they just might be the very reason why you're feeling so bad! Well that's when you start looking for answers in new directions and become willing to try looking at things in new ways.

Are women to blame
for all the porn?

As you've probably noticed, there's porn everywhere—on the Internet, in the sex shops, on DVD, and even on late night TV. Even though more women have jumped onto the porn bandwagon in recent years, there's still no doubt that porn is mainly a man thing—made for and by men.

Sometimes I wonder why it's like this. Why do so many men watch so much porn? Recently it struck me that maybe women are to blame! That maybe there's a connection between all the relationship myths that are sabotaging our happiness and the fact that more and more men are watching porn.

To understand what I'm driving at, let's take a look at a typical relationship scenario. To start with in a typical relationship, the man and the woman work really hard and are building their careers. If they have children, they have to be taken care of before and after work. They have to take the kids to and from daycare or kindergarten and then they have to shop, cook, clean, read bedtime stories and more… And then when they've finally finished all the duties of the day, most people are really tired and just want to relax a little.

But ho, it's not that simple, especially in families where the woman doesn't have a full-time career because now the woman wants the two of them to "be together". Now it's time for some "quality time" together. You know, time to talk and do stuff together. And what does the man do? Of course he agrees—because he really loves her and really wants to be a good, decent human being—even if deep down inside he just wants a little peace and quiet.

On weekends, things continue in the same vein. The man really just wants a little peace and quiet, but ho, it's not that simple. Because now they're supposed to "be together" and do the 1001 things the women's magazines say are important for the good life. Let's go look at a new kitchen and some designer furniture. Let's invite our friends for dinner or let's spend some time with the kids and so on. And the man agrees—because he really loves her and really wants to be a good, decent human being—even if deep down inside he just wants a little peace and quiet.

Then it's time for summer vacation and he thinks, Oh now maybe I can finally get a little peace and quiet. But ho, it's not that simple because the woman in his life has already made a lot of plans for the two of them. There's that exciting urban holiday to New York or Barcelona or let's visit the family on the West Coast or let's have fun with the kids at Disney World — or maybe it's time to install that new kitchen. And the man agrees again — because he really loves her and really wants to be a good, decent human being — even if deep down inside he just wants a little peace and quiet.

Then, if the man tries to weasel his way out of things and just have a little peace and quiet once in a while — well, too bad for him. Because then the woman drags him to couples therapy where he is told that if a relationship is really going to work, he must be more open and share his feelings and listen to how she feels (as if he doesn't listen to her 24 hours a day already), and that it's important for them to do things together — just for them. And since he's such a good, decent human being, he goes along with it and tries as hard as he can — even if deep down inside he just wants a little peace and quiet.

But couples therapy is just the beginning, because you know, it's important that their relationship continues to develop. So the woman in his life starts dragging him to lectures and seminars in positive thinking and clairvoyance and aura-bathing and tantra and other spiritual get-togethers where he is supposed to look deep into the eyes of some stranger and talk about his deepest feelings. And since he's such a good, decent human being, he trots along faithfully — even if deep down inside he just wants a little peace and quiet.

But then...when the woman in his life finally lets him off the hook for just a few minutes, what does he do? Well of course! He sneaks over to his computer with his heart thumping in his chest and visits porn heaven!

And heaven it is indeed. For here — in the free and uninhibited land of porn — he can be with one or several women who don't say a word and who have no expectations whatsoever and who don't threaten him with eternal damnation in relationship hell or therapy or personal development courses if he doesn't do exactly what's expected of him for a minute or two. No, here he can relax with lovely ladies who more than willingly let him shove his manhood in all three holes and finally deliver his big load right smack in their grateful shiny faces.

Ahhh... Finally a little peace and quiet....!

Are women to blame for all the porn?

PART 2

OR

Why are men such wimps?

If you read part one of this chapter, it's probably starting to dawn on you that this piece really has nothing to do with pornography. The title could just as well be "Are women to blame for all the football?" or "Are women to blame for all the time spent in front of the TV?" Or whatever else men do to have a few minutes of peace and quiet. What I'm really trying to do is shed a little light on some deeper issues.

First of all, we live in a society (and world) where both men and women are constantly being bombarded from all sides with messages about the 1001 and one things and activities we supposedly "should" have/do to live a happy life.

In this particular instance, I've chosen to look at the relationship model where it's the woman who is the standard bearer for this life of sky-high expectations. But as we will see, men in their own way are just as confused as women. If the man really wants to have some peace and quiet — and doesn't want to drive himself crazy all the time trying to achieve the dream life at the end of the women's magazines' rainbow — why doesn't he just say no and set some limits in relation to the woman in his life? Is he really such a total wimp or what?

Of course the simple answer is, Yes, he really is a total wimp. But what I would like to suggest is there are actually quite a few reasons why the man in this type of relationship ends up being such a wuss:

1) The first possible reason is that the man himself has equally bought into the idea of the 1001 things and activities we believe we must have and do to be OK and happy. He's jumped on the same bandwagon as the woman and that makes it difficult for him to say no, even if a part of him really wants to have some peace and quiet once in a while.

But if the man hasn't completely bought into the myths and deep inside doesn't want to be a part of the conspicuous consumption game, why doesn't he just say so? Why doesn't he dare say no? Why is he such a wimp?

2) To understand why he doesn't dare be honest and set some limits, we have to look a little more closely at the way he thinks. If you look back at the first part of this chapter, you'll see that the man in this type of relationship doesn't dare say no to the woman in his life because he believes in one of the oldest and greatest myths when it comes to relationships:

If you love me, you'll do what I want.

He believes that if a man loves his woman (which he does) and is a good, decent human being (which he is trying really hard to be), then he'll almost always do what his partner wants him to do.

And it's this belief—one of the most powerful myths when it comes to relationships and love—that makes it almost impossible for the man to say no.

So what do you do if you think like this (whether you're a man or a woman) and have landed in a situation like this?

The first thing you can do is question the myth. Take a good look at this age-old belief and see if it really has anything to do with reality.

Is it really true that if you love someone, you will almost always do what the other person wants?

Is it really true that if you are a good, decent human being, you will almost always do what your partner wants you to do?

If you investigate this, you will probably discover that none of these ideas are true or have anything to do with reality when it comes to relationships or human relations in general. Because what's the reality? Do you love your partner? Probably yes. And does she love you? Probably yes. Do you always want the same things? Well, probably not. Do you always agree about everything? No, probably not here either. But does this mean that you don't love and care about each other? Of course not! The two things—your love for each and your wishes and preferences in each changing moment—have nothing to do with each other. The fact that you don't always want the same things or have the same preferences has absolutely nothing to do with being a good, decent human being either.

Once you've separated these two things—your love for each other and your different desires and preferences — it makes it much easier to say no thank you when your partner asks for something that doesn't feel right to you.

But perhaps you're thinking, What if my partner still believes that if you love each other, you'll do what your partner wants? What if she pressures me to do what she wants? How can I say no?

Two good ways to say no

If your partner is pressuring you to do what she (or he) wants and you find it difficult to say no, it can be a big help to learn two of my favorite techniques for saying no. The techniques are called "fogging" and "negative inquiry" (from Manuel J. Smith's classic book on assertion called *When I say no, I feel guilty — How to cope using the skills of systematic assertive therapy*).

But a little background first: To use these two techniques effectively, it's important to understand how your partner is trying to get you to do what she wants. In her head, your partner has various beliefs about the "right" and "wrong" ways of doing things in a relationship and about what we "should" and "shouldn't" do in a relationship. So she believes that if a person breaks one of these arbitrary rules for good relationships (such as the "rule" which says that if you love me you'll do what I want) then it means that you are an inconsiderate, unloving person. What happens if you believe the same ideas and then you go and break them by saying no to your partner? Well, then both you and your partner believe that you are an inconsiderate, unloving person. How does that make you feel? Guilty of course! Which is not a very nice feeling. In fact, feeling guilty is so unpleasant that we human beings will do almost anything to avoid feeling this way — including saying yes when we really feel like saying no.

So, if your partner is non-assertive... which means that she's not good at asking directly for what she wants... This is probably because she's not good at taking "no" for an answer because she may be anxious about what a "no" might mean. If this is the case, then she will often try to manipulate you into saying yes by trying to make you feel guilty if you say "no". The way she will manipulate you is by trying to make you believe that by saying "no" you have broken one of the holy rules about relationships, which makes you an inconsiderate, unloving bastard.

Just think about it. Did you ever not want to do what your partner asked you to do — and yet ended up doing it anyway? Why did you do it? Wasn't it because he or she made you feel guilty and feel that you were a lousy human being because you violated the rules for good behavior in a relationship? What a hopeless situation to be in! If you do what feels right for you, you feel guilty. If you don't do what feels right for you and say yes to something you don't want to do, it feels uncomfortable — as if you've somehow betrayed your own integrity.

But if you look more closely you will discover that you can only feel guilty if you yourself believe in the unwritten rules for good behavior in a relationship. If you didn't believe this, there couldn't be a problem. So it turns out that in reality you're the one who's manipulating you!

Okay, so far so good. But what do you do in a real life situation when your partner asks you to do something and you honestly want to say no? What do you do if your partner still believes in certain "holy" rules for good behavior in a relationship? What do you do when she tries to manipulate you into doing something you don't want to do by criticizing you and trying to make you feel guilty?

This is where the two techniques "fogging" and "negative inquiry" can be such a great help.

Fogging

Fogging is very simple and can be quite amusing to use once you've learned how to use it. Let's say the woman in your life has asked you to do something and you've answered no. If she is non-assertive, her next move will probably be to criticize you in the hope that it will make you feel guilty so you'll do what she wants you to do. So here's what you do. Instead of defending yourself when you are criticized or entering into a long-winded discussion about the matter, you simply "fog" her. In short, this means you answer her by saying that she might be right in her criticism and that your answer is still no. Let me give you an example from my own life as an author:

WOMAN: Why don't we go for a nice picnic in the woods this weekend?
MAN: That sounds like a great idea, sweetheart, and I can't. I'm planning on working on my book this weekend.
WOMAN: But you're always working on your book on weekends. [here she's indirectly implying that there's something "wrong" with always working on a book on weekends.]
MAN: You could be right [fogging]. And I'm planning on working on my book this weekend.
WOMAN: When you work on your book you're completely lost in your own world. [Here she's indirectly implying that there's something "wrong" in getting lost in your work.]
MAN: You could be right [fogging].

WOMAN: It's been so long since we've done something together on a weekend. [Here she's indirectly implying that it's "wrong" not to have spent time together on a weekend for so long.]

MAN: You could be right [fogging].

WOMAN: You're only thinking about yourself! [Here she's indirectly implying that it's "wrong" to think about yourself.]

MAN: You could be right [fogging]. And this weekend I'm going to work on my book.

WOMAN: But what about us?

MAN: What do you mean?

WOMAN: When are we going to spend some time together?

MAN: Well let me think about it. Maybe we could go for a picnic next week, one day after work?

WOMAN: Yes that would be nice.

MAN: You could be right!

As you can see in this example of "fogging", the man doesn't defend himself when the woman criticizes him indirectly. He just acknowledges that he heard her and that he is open to the possibility that what she is saying might be true. When, for example, she says, It's been so long since we've spent time together on a weekend", he answers that she might be right. Maybe she's right and maybe she isn't. It all depends on how you look at it. And who decides when it's been a long time? What is a long time? A month? Three months? Three years? It all depends on how you look at it!

Another good thing about "fogging" is that you are also sending a strong message to your non-assertive partner that you don't mind criticism and that you don't think criticism is dangerous or something to be afraid of. You're also saying that you're quite OK with the fact that you're not perfect (whatever that means!). When you've sent this message a few times, your non-assertive partner will gradually start to understand that she won't get very far with this type of manipulation.

Negative inquiry

The next technique is called Negative Inquiry. It is even more effective when it comes to dealing with a non-assertive, manipulative woman (or man) in a skillful manner. As we just saw, the reason why someone tries to pressure her/his partner into doing what they want is that she herself is non-assertive. In other words, she has difficulty asking directly for what she wants and taking "no" for an answer. Why can't she take no for an answer? Simply because she unconsciously believes a whole slew of untrue beliefs about relationships and love and about what a "no" might mean. So, with negative inquiry, you try to gently make the other person aware of the untrue beliefs that lie behind her or his non-assertive behavior. Then when these beliefs are out in the open, you can question them or decide what to do about them. Let's try the same situation again, only this time let's deal with it using negative inquiry.

WOMAN: Why don't we go for a nice picnic in the woods this weekend?

MAN: That sounds like a great idea, sweetheart, and I can't. I'm planning on working on my book this weekend.

WOMAN: But you're always working on your book on weekends.

MAN: I don't understand. Is there something wrong with me always working on my book during the weekends? (Negative inquiry)

WOMAN: You always get completely lost in your own world when you work on your book.

MAN: I don't understand. Is there anything wrong with me getting completely lost in my own world when I'm working on my book? (Negative inquiry)

WOMAN: When you get so absorbed in your work, you forget about me.

MAN: I don't understand. Is there anything wrong with me forgetting about you when I'm working on my book? (Negative inquiry)

WOMAN: When you forget me like this, then I think you're not interested in me anymore and that maybe you don't love me anymore. (Here comes the truth — what she is really afraid of.)

MAN: That's not true darling. I do love you and I'm very interested in you. And this weekend I am planning on working on my book.

WOMAN: Do you really love me?

MAN: Yes darling, of course I do.

As you can see from this example, the woman's non-assertive behavior stemmed from the fact that she was afraid that when her partner said no to her request it meant he no longer loved her or wasn't interested in her. By using negative inquiry and questioning her statements, he finally found out what was bothering her (her basic belief) and was then able to tell her that it wasn't true. When he was absorbed in his work and forgot about his surroundings (including her) it didn't mean he wasn't interested in her or that he didn't love her.

Investigate other reasons why it's difficult to say no

In addition to the basic relationship myth "If you love me you'll do what I want", there can also be other basic beliefs that make it difficult for you to say no to your partner (or to other people in your life). A good technique for identifying and investigating these beliefs is to take a piece of paper and write at the top:

The reason I have difficulty saying no to my partner is…

Then write down all your reasons.
Here are some examples of what you might write:

If I say no, my partner will be angry.
If I say no, my partner will be hurt.
If I say no, my partner won't like me.
If I say no, my partner will leave me.
If I say no, it means I'm selfish.
I shouldn't be thinking about myself.
I should have a good reason for saying no.
I should always say yes when my partner asks for something.
I shouldn't change my mind.
I should help my partner solve his/her problems.

When you have written down the reasons why you have difficulty saying no, then investigate your statements with one of the mythbusting techniques described in Part Two of this book (see page 137). This will give you more insight into why you sometimes have difficulty saying no. Gradually with practice, it will be become easier for you to say no when your partner asks for something that doesn't feel right to you. And it will also make it easier for you to use the "fogging" and "negative inquiry" techniques described here.

RELATIONSHIP MYTHS
If you love me, you'll do what I want.
Love means you're always in agreement.

Your partner isn't
a mind reader

If you don't ask your partner for what you want, you probably won't get it. Why? Because your partner isn't a mind reader (even though many of us secretly believe this to be the case or even expect it). How can your partner possibly give you what you want, if you don't ask for it?

So, if you want something from your partner—like a hug and a kiss every time he or she comes home from work, a nice foot massage, that he or she makes dinner, a trip to the Bahamas, or whatever you happen to be dreaming about—it's certainly a good idea to ask for it.

If you're not good at asking for what you want, you might try the following exercise: Ask your partner for what you want at least three times a day. It can be for something small or something big, it doesn't matter. What's important about the exercise is that you ask for what you want directly, with no explanations or justifications; and most important of all—especially when it comes to relationships—without any kind of manipulation or threat of criticism if your partner says no. So, when you ask for something directly, you might say something like: "Sweetheart, would you give me a foot massage later?" Full stop. That's it. Don't say: "We never do anything together. You're always watching football …" Just ask for what you want, without any threat or indirect criticism.

Then try to welcome your partner's answer with open arms, whatever it is. If the answer is yes—great! If the answer is no—great! And if the answer is no, then just move on and ask someone else to give you a foot massage. Let your partner know that you love and accept him or her 100 percent whether your partner's answer is yes or no.

What do you think will make it most likely that your partner will say yes to your request: Asking for what you want directly and letting him or her know that you're happy no matter what the answer is? Or trying to force your partner to say yes (even though it may not feel right to him or her) and letting your partner know that there will be negative consequences if he or she says no?

How do you feel when somebody asks you for something in an indirect, manipulative and critical way? Does that make you feel like saying yes? Not really, right?

How do you feel when someone simply asks you for something directly and with total acceptance of your answer? Feels pretty good, huh! So good that you almost feel like saying yes…

RELATIONSHIP MYTHS

My partner should know what I'm thinking.
My partner should know how I feel.

"You're selfish if you don't do what I want!"

If you've ever had a partner who had difficulty asking directly for what she or he wants (with no form of manipulation), a partner who had a hard time accepting a "no", you've probably heard some variation of this amazing statement:

You're so selfish, because you don't do what I want.
(Or something like that).

Priceless, huh? Isn't it just amazing how confused the mind can be?

Your partner wanted you to do something to make who happy? Well, obviously to make him or her happy. And if you, God forbid, had the nerve to be so selfish as to say "no", your partner actually believed that you were being more selfish than she or he was!

Talk about amazing!

RELATIONSHIP MYTHS
I'm more selfish than my partner if I don't do what my partner wants me to do.
It's wrong to be selfish.
I shouldn't be selfish.

$f2 + s2 = rls$

f (friend) + f (friend) = f2 (friendship)
s (sex partner) + s (sex partner) = s2 (sex)
f2 (friendship) + s2 (sex) = rls (relationship)
$f2 + s2 = rls$

When you understand this universal relationship law (also known as Ray's Theory of Relationship Relativity), it becomes obvious why there are so many problems in relationships today. Basically it's because, in many instances, the men and women are not very good friends. By this, I mean they don't talk honestly to each other like good friends do. They don't accept and embrace each other unconditionally like good friends do. They don't listen openly to each other like good friends do. They don't allow each other to be exactly who they are like good friends do. They don't set each other free like good friends do. They don't support each other in following their hearts like good friends do. When they disagree, they don't respect each other like good friends do. To make matters worse, they have lots of unrealistic expectations of each other, which good friends don't usually have towards each other.

So, if a man and a woman can't even be good friends (the most essential ingredient in any relationship), is it any wonder that they have problems in what could be the most intimate relationship of all?

Can a relationship only work
if you compromise?

One of the myths you often meet in today's relationship jungle is the myth that a relationship can only work if you compromise. In other words, a relationship can only function if one or both partners sometimes do something their partner wants even if he or she really doesn't want to do it.

But is this really true? What would happen if both partners in a relationship just did what they really wanted to do—in their heart of hearts? The answer is obvious. You would have a relationship in which each partner is only doing what he or she really feels like doing.

I don't know about you, but I think this sounds like a very harmonious and peaceful way to be in a relationship!

"But," you might ask, "what if this means there are only a few things both partners feel like doing together?"

Well, what if? What if there are only a few things that both people really feel like doing together? What's wrong with that?

This leads us to another good old myth about relationships—the one that says the value of a relationship depends on how much time two people spend together. In other words, the amount of time and not the quality of the time is the determining factor.

But is this true? Is it better to be in a relationship where you spend a lot of semi-bad time together (because one or both parties are doing things they don't really want to do) than being in a relationship where you spend a little good-quality time together (because both parties are now doing what feels right for them)?

Go inside and see how this feels to you.

In fact, my experience is that one of the main reasons why so many relationships *don't work* and why there is so much confusion and unhappiness in many relationships (and why so many relationships end) is that one or both partners are compromising too much and not following their heart's desire.

What about you? Do you compromise a lot in your relationship? Do you sometimes or often do things you don't really want to do? And if the answer is yes—well why? Why do you do it? What are you afraid of? What do you believe will happen if you don't compromise? What do you believe will happen if you don't do things you don't want to do?

Or do you just go along and do things (in other words sometimes compromise) because you believe that a relationship can only work if you compromise? How would you be—and how would you feel and act—if you no longer believed in this myth? How would your relationship be? Would it work better without this belief?

There's a difference between a compromise and a transaction

Another thing that really adds fuel to the myth about relationships and compromise is the fact that so many of us confuse "compromise" with "transaction" or "agreement". Let me give you some examples of what I mean.

One of the most common types of "transactions" we all know is the commercial transaction. For example, you want to buy that nice little blue car and it costs about $15,000. The car salesman wants $15,000 and for that "price", he will give you a brand new blue car. This is a transaction. This is not a compromise. Both parties want something and both parties are willing to pay the price to get it.

Another transaction that we all experience in our life is the employee-employer transaction. For example, you want $6,000 a month and the chance to use your talents as a biochemist—and to get this you agree to show up at work every day from Monday to Friday from nine to five and do a certain job. Your employer wants a biochemist to further develop one of the company's products—and so they are willing to pay $6,000 a month to get this. This is a transaction or an agreement. It's not a compromise. Both parties want something and both are willing to pay the price to get what they want.

Another "transaction" or "agreement" that many of us enter into is the "being a parent" agreement. For example: You and your partner want to experience the joy of having a child. The "price" for this great joy is (approximately) something like this: For the next 18 years the two of you will take care of this child until the child is able to take care of him/herself (whether or not you stay together as a couple). Again, this is a transaction or an agreement. It's not a compromise. Both partners want something and both are willing to pay the price to get it. Of course you can try to back out of this "contract", but as we all know, this is a bit complicated once the baby has arrived. There's no cancelation policy when it comes to children!

What is the agreement when it comes to relationships?

But what is the agreement or "transaction" when it comes to relationships? Here things are far more unclear because when it comes to relationships we no longer have any fixed script or rules for how relationships "should" be.

It wasn't always like this. Historically speaking, it wasn't that long ago that the relationship-transaction or agreement was something like this: The woman stayed at home and cleaned and cooked and took care of the children and was the man's lover. In return, the man worked, earned money, managed the country and went to war to defend the country if necessary. It was pretty straightforward way back then. Something for something. And if a woman wasn't satisfied with this arrangement, well she was either forced into it or excluded from society — or ended up an old maid.

Today it's no longer like this (at least not in the Western world). Today, there is equality between the sexes. Women are free to work and have just as much economic and political freedom as men. Women no longer need men to take care of them. It also turns out that men are just as capable of cooking and cleaning and taking care of children and being lovers as women are. So what do we need relationships for? What is the script for relationships today?

Does the new relationship script say we have sex every Tuesday and Saturday night and go swimming on Sundays? Or does it say we do everything together (when we're not at work) or what? Or does it say we don't have any agreements or obligations at all?

The answer of course is that there isn't any fixed answer to this question today. Today most relationships — in contrast to many human transactions like commercial and job transactions — are not clearly defined. There are no clear rules as to how a relationship should be at the moment. Today relationships are a completely open arena with no limits — you can do exactly what you want.

But because most of us are not conscious of this — and because most of us still believe that a relationship is a clearly defined transaction with a fixed script — we often get into trouble when we are in a relationship. This was my experience a few years ago. After the first mad falling-in-love period, my girlfriend and I started to have all kinds of disagreements about how much time we should spend together and what we should do when we were together. I realized that a big part of our difficulty came from the fact that we had very different mental scripts when it came to how relationships "should" be. For example, my girlfriend's basic premise was that we spent all our time together (our free time) unless we agreed on something else while my basic premise was that we weren't together unless we agreed to be together. So it's easy to see how much misunderstanding this caused! It wasn't just in this area that we had problems—we each had a long list of ideas about how a relationship should be in practice and in most cases our lists just didn't match.

Unfortunately, we never sat down and talked about our expectations about relationships or agreed on them. When we finally did, we discovered that we just didn't agree on most things. It turned out that our expectations didn't match— and so the relationship ended.

Clear communication

I learned from this experience how important it is to sit down and clearly communicate your wishes and desires (as early as possible in a relationship) to each other. In practice this could mean something like:

1) Communicate clearly with yourself first. Find out who you are and what you want and don't want in a relationship. Know that what you want or don't want is 100 percent OK. You can't communicate clearly with your partner until you communicate clearly with yourself. For example, you can ask yourself things like:
   - Do you want to live with your partner or on your own? And if you want to live on your own, how often do you want to see your partner? Only on weekends? Or on weeknights too? And if you want to live together, do you want to sleep in the same bed or have separate bedrooms?
   - Do you want to have children? And if you have children, do you want to move in together or still live on your own? And how would this work?
   - If you don't live together, is it important to talk with each other every day? And what about text messages? Are they a requirement?
   - Do you want an open relationship with several partners/lovers?
   - Do you want a relationship where you don't have any agreements at all and just see each other when both of you feel like it— even if it's only once every two weeks?
   - What do you want?

Try to write down what's important for you. This is a good way of getting to know yourself.

2) Communicate your wishes and desires when it comes to relationships to your partner or potential partner. Be specific and practical. What? How much? When? Where?

3) Listen to your partner's wishes and desires when it comes to relationships. And believe what your partner or potential partner says! Don't fool yourself and think "He/she doesn't really mean that", or "He/she will change with time", or "It's just a phase he/she's going through", or one of the many other insane stories we tell ourselves about the other person instead of living in harmony with reality and accepting that the person in front of us is precisely 100 percent like he or she is and will probably NEVER change. Who would you be if you couldn't believe the thought that your partner will change? It's a pretty amazing thought, isn't it! So yes, believe what your partner tells you! This is what I call a reality check!

4) Then see if there are any or many areas where your wishes and desires match. If there are, well then maybe there really is a good basis for a relationship between you. But if there isn't, if the reality is that your wishes and expectations are very different, then it's probably a good idea to look for a more compatible partner!

RELATIONSHIP MYTHS
A relationship can only work if you compromise.
The value of a relationship depends on how much time two people spend together.
It's better to be in a relationship where you spend a lot of time together than to be in a relationship where you spend less time together.
There is a "right" and a "wrong" way to be in a relationship.
He/she will change with time.

Notes from a
sex addict's diary

There she is. Standing there in her red high heels. So sexy. I'm in a daze. Something's moving down below. What a strange phenomenon. From the red high heels to the optical nerve to movement down below... Wonder why? Hmmm. Now there's a subject for many a scientific paper. But who wants to waste time speculating over the deeper meaning of this or that when those red high heels are on their way towards me (smile)? Now they are stopping right in front of me. Inviting as hell. Hey, wow, now sound is actually coming from those red high heels. Or rather from the shapely figure that's growing out of the red high heels. Miss Red High Heels is also wearing Red Lipstick and now things are really moving (down there). What is she saying? I don't understand a word of it... other than the red lips are moving and the white teeth, tongue, mouth start a chain reaction in me that makes it totally impossible to think clearly. She's saying... Oh who the fuck cares? It's enough that those red high heels and red lips are moving closer. Now I can even smell her... Fantastic how all this red seems to smell like roses or something else indescribably sweet. It's all weaving this magic spell around me and I'm caught in her net like a poor little fly caught by a spider. Oh yes, I am the fly and you can just devour me baby...

———

Then bang! It hits me that I'm experiencing a first-class example of what those dear psychologists call "attachment hunger"... And there I go, off and running, misinterpreting the strong attraction I feel for Miss Red High Heels with the thought that a relationship with her might somehow be a wise or healthy or good thing for either of us.

Oh yeah, I've fallen into the trap once again. All the way. Boom!

But hey bro, I can still pull out before the ship really goes aground for good! Yes, yes, there's still time. Even if she's standing there swaying and luring me on with those damn red lips and those damn red high heels and all the other wonderful, shapely aspects of her that are so delicious to look at — something shifts inside me. Something healthy and wise gets the upper hand and knows that all this is just leading in one direction — straight to hell. So I smile all nice and friendly like and excuse myself. I turn resolutely away and leave, and find a few innocent-looking people who are not wearing red high heels or red lipstick that I can talk to about everything and nothing. As I stand there, I feel my inner turbulence starting to subside and begin to feel clear and easy again, right in the heart of me. Because I know I chose love for myself instead of a few seconds, a few minutes of pleasure followed by days, weeks, months and maybe even years of regret and torment!

Whew, that was a close call!

Does strong sexual attraction mean you're a good match?

One of the relationship myths that has caused me the most pain during the course of my "relationship career" is the idea that strong sexual attraction and falling in love means you're compatible and a good match. So a couple of years ago I decided to take a closer look at this idea and find out if it's really true that when you're on cloud nine and feel strong sexual attraction to someone, it means you're going to be a good match as a couple.

It didn't take me long to find the answer. When I looked back at some of my previous relationships, I could see that even though we were really attracted to each other, the reality was that we were not that good a match. Yes we might have felt blissful or even in love in the beginning, but when it came to relationships, lifestyle and interests, we often had very different views, preferences and values.

This realization was a revelation to me. Up until then, I'd been basing my choice of partner on whether or not there was a strong sexual attraction between us and not on whether or not we were a good match. Suddenly I could see the painful consequences of this misunderstanding—for me and my partners.

One of the consequences of believing that strong sexual attraction means you're a good match was that in the beginning of a new relationship, I often found myself exaggerating or only focusing on the woman's "positive" sides (oh she's so beautiful, so spiritual, and so forth) while downplaying or even ignoring her more "negative" sides. For example, I would overlook the sudden unkind remark that made me feel uncomfortable and instead sweep it under the carpet because I was so much in love. Or I'd accept an action or actions on her part that I'd never accept in anyone else. But in her case, because the attraction was so strong, I'd let it slide. I have to admit that if I had been totally honest with myself, the truth was I already knew on the very first date, in the very first five minutes or so of our conversation, why the relationship would sooner or later become unworkable. Yes it's true, I actually knew from the very beginning the reasons why we would not be a good match.

But because I was so infatuated and innocently believed that strong sexual attraction means you're a good match, I ignored reality. The result was almost always the same. As soon as the intoxication of falling in love began to wear off and the reality began to set in, it would become more and more painful for me to stay in the relationship. Then, the long, difficult battle to extricate myself would begin.

Find your core values

So if strong sexual attraction and falling in love don't necessarily mean you're a good match, what does? What makes two people a good match?

One of the things that make two people a good match is that they have the same "core" values. By having the same core values, I don't mean being the same personality type or having the same education or working in the same field. I mean you have the same basic attitudes when it comes to what's important in life, not least what's important when it comes to relationships.

One of the reasons why many relationships get into serious trouble is that the man and the woman don't have the same core values. A "mismatch" like this usually spells trouble because most people live according to their core values — and usually unconsciously expect their partners to do so too. This can be problematic when these core values don't match. Let's take an example. Let's say one of your core values is "freedom" while your partner's core values are "security and feeling safe". Obviously this can make your relationship problematic because you will both unconsciously be expecting the other to behave in a manner that is in conflict with his or her core value or values. So when you are faithful to your core value and give yourself and your partner lots of "freedom", your partner may get upset and feel insecure because his/her core values of "security and feeling safe" are not being met or are threatened. The opposite is true too. When your partner tries to live in harmony with his/her core value and strives for "security" for example, by wanting clear agreements on how you do things, the "freedom-loving" partner feels stifled and inhibited. You feel your core value of "freedom" is being threatened. So this is why it is so important to be more aware of what you and your partner's (or a potential partner's) core values are.

My former girlfriend, sexologist and couples therapist Joan Ørting, has developed a good exercise to help us become more aware of our core values when it comes to relationships. I suggest you give this exercise a try, it can be really interesting. Ask yourself the following questions and answer as honestly as you can.

QUESTION: What is most important for you in a relationship?
ANSWER: That my partner accepts me and loves me unconditionally.
QUESTION: How does it make you feel when your partner accepts you and loves you unconditionally?
ANSWER: It makes me feel SAFE.
CONCLUSION: So feeling SAFE is one of your core values.

Repeat the questions until you identify 3-5 of your main core values. Once you've done this, prioritize the values so that you end up with a list that looks like this:

My core values when it comes to relationships:
    1) Feeling safe
    2) Being together
    3) Joy

Or perhaps you'll come up with a list of core values that looks like this:
    1) Freedom
    2) Adventure
    3) Being together

Becoming aware of your core values can be a really big help when it comes to determining if you and a potential partner are a good match. If you're already in a relationship and are having problems, it may be because your core values do not match. So it can also be helpful to do this exercise with your partner and then talk about what your respective core values are. Understanding how your core values differ can make it easier to communicate with each other in the future.

Identify your "Attachment Fetish Person"

Here's another interesting way of exploring why two people may or may not be a good match.

Once I began to realize that "strong sexual attraction" doesn't necessarily mean you're a good match, another question arose: "If strong sexual attraction doesn't necessarily mean you're a good match, then why does this strong attraction arise in the first place? How come I'm so attracted to someone who might not be good for me?"

Also "How come I keep falling for a certain type—over and over again—even though this type of person is obviously not a good match for me?"

When I looked back at the partners I've had and the women I've been attracted to, I could see that there were often specific physical traits and personalities that I seemed to fall for. I could also see that what attracted me wasn't necessarily the same as what attracted other men.

Fascinating, isn't it?

I bet there's a certain type of man or woman who turns you on too. Maybe you fall for the Brad Pitt type with the muscular body and the charming, boyish smile? Or perhaps you're into the more sensitive, artistic Johnny Depp type? If you're a guy, maybe you go for the sexy, dangerous Angelina Jolie types? Or do you prefer the quiet, gentle Gwyneth Paltrow type? If you think about it, you can probably identify the type you tend to be attracted to.

Here's a fun and interesting exercise that can help you understand what attracts you more clearly:

- Take a sheet of paper and divide it into three columns. In the left column, write the names of all the partners you've had in your life (including your current partner if you have one).

- In the middle column, write next to each partner's name a few key words about his or her physical appearance. For example: Thin, tall, dark complexion, beautiful face, long wavy hair, laid-back clothes.

- In the right column, next to each partner's name write a few key words about this person's personality. For example: Contemplative, introverted, artistic, loner, insecure, slightly self-destructive. Or reckless, talkative, enthusiastic, passionate.

- Once you've done this for all your partners, go through the middle and right hand columns and circle the traits — both physical and personality-wise — that occur more than once. Now look at what you have circled. You have just identified the recurring traits. What did you find? Maybe you find that you have a tendency to fall for thin, sensitive men who are introverted and artistic, but who are also insecure and a little self-destructive. Or perhaps you fall for voluptuous, exotic women who can be wild and impulsive, but also bitchy.

These recurring personality traits and physical characteristics make up your "Attachment Fetish Person". ("Attachment Fetish Person" is a psychological term for the particular type of woman or man who you have a tendency to fall for.

For more about this interesting phenomenon, see Howard M. Halpern's fascinating book *How to Break Your Addiction to a Person*.)

Precisely why each of us has a tendency to be attracted to a particular type of man or woman is a very complex question. But regardless of the deeper reasons for our attraction to a particular type of person, the qualities we are attracted to are a good indication of what we are seeking in our lives. So let's say you have a tendency to be attracted to wild, impulsive women. This is probably a sign that on some level, you would like more impulsiveness and adventure in your life. If you're attracted to the quieter, more introverted types, it's probably a sign that on some level you'd like more peace and quiet in your life!

Cultivate the qualities you're attracted to

OK. So now you know that these qualities are something you would like to have more of in your life, how can you go about getting more of these qualities in your life — whether or not you have a partner?

Here's a good way to cultivate more of the qualities you want in your life:

1) For each quality you are attracted to, find at least three concrete examples of how you already have this quality in your life. In reality, when you are attracted to some characteristic in another person, it is a reflection of a quality or characteristic you already possess. If you didn't have it, you wouldn't be able to see it. He or she is just reflecting back to you something you already have within, even though at the moment, this quality may not be so developed or visible to you. (It might even be suppressed.)

So if one of the qualities or characteristics you are attracted to in others is "adventurous and reckless", then try to find three concrete examples of how you already have this quality. For example:
   A) That time you decided to go on a trip to Paris all by yourself because you wanted to go to the clubs on the Left Bank,
   B) When you are all by yourself dancing with the curtains drawn,
   C) When you're out running in the woods with no particular plan or direction.

Once you have identified situations in your life where you already have these qualities you want, you can cultivate them even more.

2) If you have difficulty finding a particular quality in yourself and would like to

experience more of it, you can also ask yourself what you can do to cultivate more of this quality in your life. So again if you want to experience more of that "adventurous" feeling, maybe it would be a good idea to allow yourself to try something new — like learning to tango! Or going to a poetry slam and reading one of your own creations… or traveling to the Outer Hebrides to feel the wild wind of the Atlantic Ocean in your hair…

Your Attachment Fetish Person can also be a mirror of what you dislike!

If you look a little more closely at your "Attachment Fetish Person" you'll probably also discover that not only does the person have certain qualities you are drawn towards and like but he or she may also have qualities or characteristics you really dislike!

Maybe the person you fall for also has a tendency to become aggressive when you don't do what they want. Maybe he or she is someone who criticizes you and tries to force you to do things that don't feel right to you. These less attractive character traits can also be a mirror of what's going on inside you. A mirror which is showing the part of you that treats you aggressively and tries to get you to do things that don't feel right to you. Because why else would you allow yourself to be with someone who treats you like that? What is it about you that is willing to put up with that kind of behavior?

If you can see or have the feeling that you are being run by some unhealthy thought pattern like the one mentioned above, what can you do about it? Fortunately there are many good techniques which can help you to identify and free yourself from such unhealthy behavior. One of the best methods is The Work of Byron Katie. For more about this simple, but very effective method, see page 149 in Part Two of this book.

RELATIONSHIP MYTH
Strong sexual attraction means you're a good match.

Is it better to be in a relationship than to be single?

If you happen to be single, how many times have people commented: "I'm sure you'll meet somebody soon" or "There's plenty of fish in the sea" or "Have you tried this or that dating site"?

If you're single, when was the last time somebody said: "Well, congratulations! I'm so happy for you. It's about time too. May you live single happily ever after!"

Probably never, right!

If you're in a relationship, when was the last time somebody said to you: "Don't worry, you'll probably soon be single again. Sooner or later all relationships come to an end" or "Poor you, I really feel for you. Is there anything I can do for you?" or "Wow, you must really need a little alone time."

Probably never, right!

There are gazillions of dating sites on the Internet that are all about finding a partner, but how many Internet sites are there about how to become single?

Like....

www.50waystoleaveyourlover.com

or

www.howtobecomesinglefast.com

Who knows? Maybe they'd be big hits.

RELATIONSHIP MYTH
It's better to be in a relationship than to be single.

Facts about singles

- For the first time ever the majority of American women are single — 51 percent.
- 96 million people in the United States (43 percent of all Americans over the age of 18) are single. More than every fourth American household (27 percent) is inhabited by a person who lives alone.
- There are 3.8 million singles in New York City alone.
- If you went on a date with a new person every day of the week, 52 weeks of the year, for the next 50 years, you will have dated a total of 18,250 men or women. That's still less than 0.5 percent of the single population in New York City!

Source:
The U.S. Census Bureau and Council on Contemporary Families

Fed up with the traditional relationship model?

The last few years I've noticed that some of the singles in my circle of friends (both men and women) don't seem to have any particular desire to find new partners. A few seem to have more or less completely given up the thought that it is possible for them to find a partner who they'd be compatible with.

I've wondered more than once — how can this be? Why do some people seem to be wondering if they're cut out for this whole relationship thing? Is it because they really don't want to be in a relationship? Is it because when push comes to shove, they are afraid of "making a commitment"? Is it because they just haven't found the "right" person yet? Or is there a completely other reason? What if their waning interest in having a regular partner has nothing to do with not wanting a partner? What if it's because the traditional relationship model just doesn't work for them?

When I talk to some of the singles I know who are wondering if being in a relationship is really something for them, I've discovered something interesting. It seems that the problem for many is not that they don't want a partner, but rather that they simply don't want any of the following three variations of the traditional relationship that we have been brainwashed to believe are the only correct way of doing things:

1) A relationship where each person lives on their own
2) A relationship where two people live together
3) A relationship where two people live together and have children

Since most of us believe that the three above variations of the traditional model are the only options, some of us are starting to feel that having a relationship might not be the right thing for us.

But what if it's not true that the traditional relationship models are the only options? What if there are many more ways of being in a relationship? What if there are countless creative ways of being in a relationship which you can adjust and adapt until there is one that exactly fits your needs and the way you live your life? What if there were no limits to the ways in which people can design their relationships? Here are some examples of how things could be:

- We don't live together and don't see each other on weekdays but on weekends I stay at your place.
- We live together but have two bedrooms so we don't have to sleep together every night.
- We don't live together and are first and foremost good friends. Sometimes, when we feel like it, we have sex together.
- Our basic agreement is that we don't have any fixed agreements about anything and just see each other when we both feel like it (even if this is only once every 14 days or once a month).
- One partner's need for companionship is greater than the other so we agree that it's OK for that person to have two or three partners.
- We agree on a time limit for the relationship, for example, we'll be together for a month or for three months.
- We take "relationship leave" or a "relationship sabbatical" (like at the workplace or at university) where we take a "leave of absence" from the relationship for an agreed period of time.
- We are partners and have a child together, but we each live on our own, a couple of blocks away. The child lives with the mother all of the time and the father visits.
- We are partners and have a child together, but we each live on our own, a couple of blocks away. The child lives with the father all of the time, and the mother visits.
- We are partners and have a child together, but we each live on our own, a couple of blocks away. We take turns having the child.
- And any other creative combination that you can think up that two people can agree upon!

Because in reality, a relationship is not some predefined thing but an agreement that two people negotiate and agree upon — just like when you go to a job interview or join any other type of project. So why not sit down at the table and negotiate with your partner. Present your wishes and listen to your partner's wishes and see if you can't agree upon a solution that satisfies both of you.

Remember, do this as early as possible in your relationship! I can see that one of the classic "mistakes" I've made was believing that falling in love and strong sexual attraction are the same as being compatible with someone. Then when the first rush of enchantment began to fade, we suddenly discovered the truth. Oops… that yes, even if we really were attracted to each other, we just didn't want the same things when it came to having a relationship!

So if you are one of those people who sometimes wonder if having a relationship is something for you, maybe you should take a new look at the concept of relationships. Maybe it's not that relationships are not for you, but that the traditional relationship models are just too limiting!

RELATIONSHIP MYTHS
The traditional relationship model is the only option.
The traditional relationship model is the only right way to do things.
There is a "right" and a "wrong" way to be in a relationship.

Wanted:
A quarter of a relationship!

One day I was talking to a friend of mine about the many new ways of being in a relationship besides the traditional relationship models we've had for so many generations. New ways like living together and having two bedrooms so the partners don't have to sleep together every night. Or a relationship in which one of the partners has two partners because her or his need for companionship is greater than his or her partner's.

When I said this, my friend exclaimed, "Tim, wouldn't you just love that — having two girlfriends?"

I just laughed.

"Me?" I said, "No way! I don't even have enough time or space in my life for one girlfriend — much less two! What I'd really like is a quarter of a girlfriend!"

"A quarter of a girlfriend?" my friend asked. "But if that's the case, why not just get yourself a mistress?"

"No," I said. "That's not the same. With a mistress basically all you do is have sex. I don't just want that. I want someone I can share the other good things you share with a girlfriend. You know like friendship, stimulating conversation, love and warmth, mutual support, doing things together — as well as sleeping together and having sex. But I only want it a quarter of the time. So I guess what I'm really saying is I want the same quality as I'd get with a full-time girlfriend or partner, but much less quantity!"

Does this sound like you? Would you also like to have a partner you can share the good things one shares with a full-time partner — but only in smaller doses? In other words, would you really like a quarter of a partner too?

Recently I saw a program on TV about people who were in unconventional relationships. One of them was a "couple" that consisted of one woman and two men. The woman was what my friends and I would call "high-maintenance" because she had lots of demands and expectations to a relationship, especially when it came to how much time the partners spend together. The two men on the other hand did not want to spend so much time with a woman because their lives were so full to begin with, but they both wanted a girlfriend. When interviewed, both men said they loved this woman but that she was simply was too exhausting for one man to handle! So, the merry threesome had come up with a solution that fulfilled the wishes of all three of them. Both men were in the relationship with this woman and they took turns spending time with her! An ingenious solution indeed because in this way, the woman got to spend a lot of time with a partner (which was what she wanted) and the men got to spend time (but less time) with a partner, which was also what they wanted.

Creative indeed! And why shouldn't we be?

So maybe we should consider creating some new categories on the dating sites such as:

WANTED: *A full-time relationship*
WANTED: *A half of a relationship*
WANTED: *A quarter of a relationship!*

"Do you want to be my girlfriend for three months?"

Here's another idea for a new way of having a relationship that might be really healthy and fun to try. *A fixed-term relationship. For example for three months.* There are many advantages to a relationship model like this:

- You live much more in the now and can be grateful for what you have right now instead of regarding what you have now as a stepping stone to some future destination (which so many people unfortunately do). So, instead of constantly worrying about where this relationship is going, you could enjoy it for what it is right now. Just think about it for a moment. If you really knew that you and your partner would only be together for three months, wouldn't you enjoy the person and the relationship much more and be much more present in the now?

- Another good thing about a fixed-term relationship would be you won't be disappointed or feel you've wasted time, if after three months it turns out that you or the other person does not want to continue the relationship. Since you both already agreed from the start that the relationship was only going to last three months, it will be easier to stop and you won't feel you have so much to "lose" if you decide not to continue.

- When the three months are over, you can take a short break — say for a month — so each of you has time to consider whether or not he or she wants to sign up for another three months! If it turns out you're not that good a match, then you can be grateful for the three months you shared and just move on. If it turns out that you're a good match, well then you can just renew your agreement. In this way, you are also making sure that the relationship never goes on auto-pilot and gets boring, because by regularly taking breaks from each other you are continually re-evaluating the relationship and allowing yourself to ask if you really want to continue and/or make changes.

So maybe next time you meet someone you really like, you should get down on your knees, look her straight in the eyes and say: "Would you like to be my girlfriend for three months?"

Going to a relationship
interview with Tim Ray

When a company is looking for a new employee, candidates usually go through one or more job interviews to determine whether the candidate is the right person for the job. Things like the candidate's background, educational credentials, and previous work experience are explored in detail, as well as the responsibilities and challenges of the new job, and the company values and vision. The candidate will be asked what he or she can contribute to the company and in return, the company may offer good career advancement potential. Finally, there may be negotiations about salary, perks, job training, etc.

So I've been thinking, why don't we evaluate people just as carefully when we're looking for new partners? Why don't we invite potential candidates for the job as a new partner to "relationship" interviews and find out whether he or she is the right person for the job!

Not a bad idea, right?

Here are some of the things I might ask a woman who comes to be interviewed for the job of being my new girlfriend:

"So you are interested in the job of being my new girlfriend. Do you realize that at the moment this is only a part-time job? So tell me, how do you feel about flexible working hours?"

"I presume that you have carefully studied the job description and realize that this is a rather unusual job with some unusual responsibilities and challenges… and that the job as my girlfriend will probably involve quite a lot of inner work…"

"What are your qualifications for the job? Why do you believe that you are the right person for me? I can see from your CV that you have some previous relationship experience—and I'm happy to see you have some international relationship experience too. But do you have any experience in having a boyfriend like me?"

"What can you contribute to my life? Can you tell me briefly why I should choose you for the job of my girlfriend?"

"How would you describe your strengths and weaknesses when it comes to relationships?"

"I can see that your last relationship with John ended rather abruptly... What happened there? I can also see from your CV that you've had four different relationships in the last seven years."

"Hmm, I can see that the competition clause with your last boyfriend expired several months ago, so you are clear as far as he is concerned..."

"The recommendation from your ex-boyfriend Martin is really quite amazing... Would you mind if I call him and have a little chat with him about you?"

"As for me, I can offer you an exciting and unconventional relationship that will give you a great deal of freedom... and there will be plenty of opportunity for further development which you will be able to take with you to any new relationship you might have in the future... Plus, I would like to add that we usually have a lot of fun in my relationships..."

"I will not hide from you the fact that there are many candidates for the job... but you are one of the best I've met so far...

"How would you feel about starting as a trainee for the job as my girlfriend? It would give you the opportunity to see what the job is all about and what the potential is... We could start with a trial period of say three months and see how it goes..."

OK, I realize that subjecting a potential partner to this kind of "third degree interrogation" may not be the most romantic thing for a first date! But still, we use so much time and energy planning our educating, our career, our dreams and goals in life, why don't we do just a little of the same when it comes to what we really want in our relationships? Instead of jumping into bed with the first attractive person you meet at the disco and then waking up the next morning married with three kids!?

What happens to the hero and heroine AFTER they finally get each other?

Fascinating how romantic comedies never tell you anything about what happens AFTER the hero and heroine finally get each other...

So how about STARTING a "Rom-Com" the very moment our dear hero and heroine finally get each other (after of course having passed through fire and brimstone and endless tribulations). The very first scene in the movie would be the one you usually see at the end, with the hero and heroine running in slow-motion towards each other across a flowery meadow, with violins playing in the background, as they finally fall into each other's arms, kissing madly, tenderly, and then ...

CUT to the next scene. After several weeks of hot, well-earned marathon sex, it's back to everyday life for our dear hero and heroine. So what are they going to do now? (There is after all, a limit to how much sex any human being can have. Even the sweetest dessert becomes sickening if you eat it for breakfast, lunch and dinner.) Then of course there's the other question. Can our handsome hero and ravishing heroine actually figure out how to live with each other now that their lives are no longer filled with almost insurmountable obstacles, complicated intrigues, evil stepmothers, scheming stepsisters, jealous husbands, deadly family rivalries or impending world doom?

The first sign of trouble in paradise arises when the heroine invites the hero to join her for dinner with her family (often a decisive moment in any relationship!). This is the first time our dear hero faces a real relationship dilemma. You see even though he promised to go through fire and water and even give up his life for the woman he loves, the reality is he already said yes to go on a fishing trip with his buddies this particular weekend. So, he politely says no thank you to his dear woman. And what happens? Unfortunately our dear heroine is very hurt and disappointed (because she believes in the myth that *"If you love me, you'll do what I want"*), and our couple has their first argument. "But, I thought you loved me?" says our heroine in tears. "But I do love you, sweetheart," replies our hero. "Then why won't you go with me for dinner at my parents' house this weekend? The whole family is going to be there…" she sniffles. Now our hero is really in a jam and in the end he reluctantly agrees because he believes in the myth that *"a relationship can only work if you compromise"*.

After the family get-together, our dear hero and heroine get into yet another argument — this time about the future. During dinner, the question of children came up and our hero declared that he wanted to finish his MBA first and get his career going a bit more before he started a family — something that our dear heroine is not altogether pleased with. And on their way home in the car she hits him with those "Five Deadly Words" that are often like dark clouds before the sun in so many otherwise happy relationships: "Where-Is-This-Relationship-Going?" she says slowly and ominously. And there you have it… those Five Deadly Words. Why did she do it? Why did she summon those dark, angry clouds before the sun? Because she believes the relationship myth: *"We have a future together. This moment is only a stepping stone to some future destination"*.

After a day of such confusion, arguing and disappointment (because of our dear hero and heroine's belief in our many collective relationship myths), their sexual desire is somewhat low and our dear couple spends their first night together without hot, mind-blowing sex. So it goes, day after day, until our hero starts to spend more and more time at work and less and less time with our heroine. They are drifting apart. Then one day our dear heroine discovers that our hero is having an affair with that sexy project manager from iCube Electronics. This lands them at their first session with a sexologist who gives them good advice as to how they can spice up their sex life and become more intimate again. But what our dear hero, heroine and sexologist do not suspect is that the problems our dear hero and heroine are having, have nothing to do with their sex life at all! In fact, their problems are caused by their innocent and unconscious belief in the 101 relationship myths that sabotage our happiness.

So in the end, after trying to kick start their lackluster sex life with the Kama Sutra, Tantra, S/M and fifteen different types of blowjobs in the great outdoors, our dear hero and heroine part ways. And there we find them — him sitting all alone and her sitting all alone in some bar, deeply disappointed and wondering how something that started so blissfully could end so miserably. Yes, now they're depressed because they also believe in the relationship myth that *"a relationship is only a success if it lasts until death do us part"*!

So how about a movie like this? Do you think a romantic comedy (or rather tragedy) like this would have the slightest chance in Hollywood? Or do you reckon most of us would rather live in the illusion that the couples we see embracing and kissing so passionately at the end of those movies really do live happily ever after?

RELATIONSHIP MYTHS
They lived happily ever after.
Other couples are so much happier than we are.

The only thing you can
experience in your relationship
is your own thinking

Have you ever asked yourself why you want to be in a relationship? If you have, or if you ask yourself now, you'll probably discover that the answer is because you want to be happy. That's what we all want—what everyone wants—to be happy. That is precisely what this book is about. How you can live a happy life. By that I mean how you can be happy:

- No matter what your partner says or does (or doesn't say or do!)
- No matter what happens or doesn't happen in your relationship
- Whether you are with your partner or not

When you read this you might think: "Whoa… Wait a minute there—that's just not possible! You can't be happy regardless of what's going on in your relationship! It's simply not possible and it's inhuman to boot!"

I would say, well yes, you're right. As long as you believe all your thoughts about your relationship and about your partner, you are right, it's impossible. As long as you believe in all the universal myths about relationships and love, then yes again, you are definitely right. It's just not possible to be happy no matter what happens in your relationship when you believe this kind of thinking.

This is because, as I wrote in the Introduction, it is your thinking that determines your experience of your life. It is your thinking that determines how you experience your relationship and your partner. It's also your thinking that determines whether you are happy or unhappy in your relationship—not your partner or your current relationship status.

Now I realize that this might sound radical, especially because most of us have been taught (programmed) from our early childhood to believe the opposite is true. We have been told, over and over again that our happiness (or unhappiness) is dependent on outside circumstances such as our partner or what our partner says and does (or rather *doesn't* say or do!).

But is this really true? Is it really true that our happiness depends on outer circumstances? Is it really true that our happiness depends on our relationship and on the way our partners behave? Is it true what our collective myths tell us about the nature of relationships?

This is a rather important question, isn't it? Especially since your happiness and mine are at stake!

So let's take a closer look at this very important question.

Why do you sometimes feel happy in your relationship and why do you sometimes feel unhappy and upset? Is it because of your partner or what?

In order to get a little more clarity on this very important issue, let's look at what the reality is when it comes to this thing called relationships. Let's look at what the reality is when it comes to your relationship and the relationships of every other man and woman on the planet. By doing this, it will be easier for you to understand why you sometimes feel happy in your relationship and sometimes quite unhappy.

The truth about relationships

If you look carefully at what's going on, you will see that when it comes to your relationship and your partner at the moment, the reality is your relationship is exactly the way it is right now. That is the reality or the truth of the matter. Plain and simple. Now this is not a question about right or wrong or how things "should" or "shouldn't" be. I'm just talking about the reality of what is when it comes to you and your relationship right now. Not what you think it "should" be. Not what you think it "could" be. Not what you hope it will be. But simply what it is right now.

So what is the reality right now when it comes to you and relationships? It's actually quite simple when you look at it this way. The reality is that right now you are either in a relationship or you're not. That's reality. Plain and simple. Right now, at this very moment, there's nothing you can do about it. Yes, of course if you're single, you can try to find a partner and go to the nearest dating site or hang out at a singles club. Maybe you'll find someone and maybe you won't, but the reality is that right now you are either single or you're in a relationship. That's it. Plain and simple.

If you are in a relationship, then the reality is that right now you are either with your partner or you're not. Again that's reality. Plain and simple. If you're not with your partner at the moment and would like to be, well, then, you can call him and ask him if he wants to come over or ask him to come home if you live together. Maybe he will, maybe he won't. But right now, in this moment, the reality is that you're not with your partner. Or else you are.

If you are in a relationship, then the reality is also that your partner is exactly the way he or she happens to be. That means your partner says and does exactly what he or she happens to say or do (or *doesn't* say or do!). He either picks his nose or he doesn't. He either helps with the dishes or he doesn't. He either watches a lot of TV or he doesn't. He's either interested in self-help and personal development or he's not. He's either the type who brings you flowers and chocolate or he isn't. That is also the reality right now. Plain and simple. Your partner is the way he or she happens to be. Not the way you think he or she "should" be. Not the way you hope or believe or expect him or her to be, but simply the way he or she is. That's the reality of it. Yes, of course you can ask your partner for what you want, and yes, of course you can suggest changes if you think there's a better way of doing things. But when all is said and done, when you've done whatever you can do, you're still left with the reality of the way things are right now. Which is that your partner is exactly the way your partner is right now.

That's reality. That's the truth about your relationship — and about every relationship. It is the way it is.

But what about happiness?

Well, what about it?

If you take a closer look at what you are thinking (for example, about your partner) and at the cause-and-effect-relationship between your thinking and your experience, you will also discover that you can only be unhappy if you believe your partner should be different than the way he or she really is. In other words, when you believe that reality — for example the way your partner is right now — should be different than it is.

Every time you believe that reality should be different than it is right now, you suffer. It's actually that simple. So every time you feel unhappy in your relationship you can know that you are resisting the reality. You can know that your thinking is not in harmony with the way things are.

Because as we just saw, when it comes to you and relationships, the way it is…is the way it is. That's reality. You're either single or in a relationship. You're either with your partner right now or not. Your partner either does this or does that. That's the way of it right now. Every time you believe that things should be different than they are, every time you believe that your relationship or your partner should be different than he or she is right now, you get frustrated and upset.

So if you believe the thought that your partner shouldn't spend so much time surfing the Internet—and the reality is that he does (no matter how many times you asked him not to)—what happens? You feel angry and frustrated because you are resisting what is. So maybe you lash out at him or sneer at him; maybe you are distant and cold. In short: YOU become unhappy. YOU feel bad.

So how would you feel if you couldn't believe the thought that your partner shouldn't spend so much time surfing the Internet? (This doesn't mean you can't ask him for what you want. You can.) But if he continues to do what he does, how would you feel if you accepted the reality, which is you have a partner who spends a lot of time surfing the Internet (or anyway more time than you think he should)? How would you feel if you saw and accepted the reality? Wouldn't you feel a lot more peaceful? Wouldn't you feel more relaxed? Wouldn't you feel less resistance to what's going on and maybe more love too? How would that affect your relationship? How would that affect the way you treat your partner? Can you find that in yourself? Maybe you'd be a just little more lighthearted in your interactions with your partner, a little more joyous... In short: Maybe YOU'D feel better, happier. (Again, this doesn't mean that you can't have preferences and walk away if you really don't want a partner who spends so much time at the computer. This doesn't mean you can't leave and try to find a partner who is more compatible with your preferences.)

It all depends on your thinking

When you look at the example above, you'll see that no matter how you react, the reality of the situation and your partner is 100 percent the same. When you believe your partner shouldn't spend so much time at his computer, the reality is the same—he does spend a lot of time (or more time than you think he should be spending). When you don't believe your thinking and accept how much time he spends at his computer, the reality is still the same—he's still spending the same amount of time there. No matter how you look at it, the reality is exactly the same. The only difference is YOU. Either you feel frustrated and unhappy or you feel relaxed and happy.

So you have the same reality with two very different interpretations. As a result, you have two very different life experiences. That's it. The only difference is your thinking. It's your interpretation that determines how you feel about the time your partner spends at the computer. It's your thinking that determines whether you feel bad about it or not—not what your partner does or doesn't do.

The same goes for any other situation you may experience in your relationship. If your partner says or does something, it's your thinking that determines how you experience what your partner says or does—not what your partner is actually saying or doing.

If you don't believe this is true, just take a look at the people around you. Notice how some people are perfectly fine with a partner who behaves the way your partner behaves, while others are really upset by the same behavior. So what's the difference? Only our interpretation of what's going on.

If your partner leaves you or is together with someone else, it's still your thinking which determines how you feel about the situation and not the fact that your partner has left or is with someone else. Because again, some people brush off something like that easily while others fall into the deepest despair. Again, what's the difference? Only your interpretation. If you happen to be single, again it's your thinking that determines how you feel about being single —and not the fact that you are single. Because again, some people enjoy being single while others really have a hard time with it. So again, it's our thinking that determines how we react—not our partner or lack of one.

Many people find this hard to understand at first because most of us have been taught from childhood to believe that outer circumstances are the cause of the way we feel. But if you carefully examine what's going on and understand the way your mind works, you will see that it's not outer circumstances which determine the way you feel at all! It's your thinking and your interpretation of what's going on that is the cause of the way you feel. And only always.

The key to your happiness is in you

If you understand this, then you can also understand why I said in the beginning of this chapter that it is possible to be happy no matter what is happening in your relationship. This is true because the cause of your happiness or unhappiness is your own thinking—not outer circumstances or your partner. If you think deeply about this, you will also see that this is actually good news. Very good news! Because it means that the key to your happiness lies within YOU! Yes—in YOU! Not with your partner!

This is pretty amazing when you think about it.

Because it makes you responsible for you—and not your partner!

Just think how terrible it would be if the opposite was true! Just think about how terrible it would be if your partner really was responsible for your happiness! Just think about what a nervous wreck you'd be if this really was the case.

(Which also makes it easier to understand why so many people are so unhappy in their relationships! Yes, because they actually do believe that their happiness is dependent on what their partners do or don't do... and ouch! That really hurts.)

So, yes, the "Devil" (our confused thinking) sure has done a number on us!

But fortunately for us, we can wake up! We can wake up and see that in reality, the cause of our happiness or unhappiness has nothing to do with outer circumstances or with our partners, but with our own thinking. This is good news because you can do something about your own thinking. You can become aware of your thinking and then, if you are feeling unhappy, you can investigate your thoughts and work with them and even change them so that you feel better. By this, I mean you can bring your thinking more into harmony with reality and learn to see and accept the things which are beyond your control — things like your partner. The more you do this, the more peace and happiness you will experience in your relationship. It's really very simple.

This doesn't mean you can't strive to find the partner of your dreams or ask your present partner for what you want. No, not at all. But whether you find your dream partner and whether your partner does what you want or not is ultimately beyond your control. The only thing that is within your control is your own thinking. Fortunately for all of us, this truth is empowering... because our thinking is the key to our happiness.

Living in harmony with reality is not the same as being passive

When people hear this information for the first time, they sometimes say: "But does this mean I should just be passive? That I can't have any wishes and preferences when it comes to relationships? That I should just accept things the way they are, and not actively work to improve things or create the life or relationship I want?"

The answer is absolutely no! It doesn't mean that at all. If the reality is that your partner doesn't do what you want, what's the most constructive and healthy attitude you can take towards that reality? Is it:

RESISTANCE: "I've asked my partner for what I want over and over again and he always says no. He's such a jerk—he's so selfish. All he thinks about is himself. If he really loved me, he'd do what I want. So I guess he doesn't love me. If he did, he would do what I want."

ACCEPTANCE: "I've asked my partner for what I want over and over again and he keeps saying no. So, what do I do now? I could try asking him again next week or I could ask someone else for what I want. Or I could try to give myself what I want. That might be interesting. There are so many exciting options!"

Or if your partner left you, you could react with:

RESISTANCE: "Oh my God, how could this happen to me? My partner left me! This shouldn't be happening. She shouldn't have left me, it's not fair. How could she do this to me! I can't stand it! I can't stand being on my own. This is terrible."

ACCEPTANCE: "My partner left me. It feels quite empty, but it's an interesting new development. Not quite what I expected. There's such a lot of extra space suddenly. Actually, it's pretty exciting. I can't wait to see what new and interesting things and people flow into all this new space? I think I'll start taking salsa lessons — never know who you'll meet."

Or if you're single, you could react with:

RESISTANCE: "I'm single and it's terrible. I can't stand being alone. I'll never find a new partner. I'll be alone for the rest of my days. Oh my God, my next date better be a good one or I don't know what I'll do."

ACCEPTANCE: "I'm single now and it's an interesting, new situation indeed! Why is my life better because I'm single? Hmmm… Well, suddenly I have so much more time for myself. I wonder what's the best and most exciting way I can use all this new time? There are so many possibilities… Wow. It'll be interesting to see if I meet someone new."

As you can see from the above examples, the reality in all these cases is the same. Something happens and then you're either at war with the situation or you're living in harmony with it. The reality is just the way it is. You've asked your partner for what you want and he said no. Or your partner has left you. Or you're single, and there's nothing you can do about it at the moment. That's the way your reality is right now. You can stomp and holler and resist all you want, but it won't change the situation.

Or you can accept what's going on.

Which reaction do you think is the most constructive? As you can see from the above, when you resist, it's not constructive at all (quite contrary to what many believe)—actually it's quite destructive and it closes you down to any possible joy and new possibilities. Acceptance, on the other hand, makes life friendlier (for you) because it welcomes reality and makes you open to the exciting new possibilities the present situation may bring.

RELATIONSHIP MYTHS
My happiness is dependent on my partner.
My happiness is dependent on outer circumstances.

Who would your partner
be if you got your way?

Most of us have lots of ideas about how we'd like our partners to be — ideas about what he or she "should" say or do (or not say or not do) so that we can be happy, ideas about how they should change or live their lives, ideas about what is right or wrong for them — and so on.

But you may have noticed that no matter how hard we try, the reality is that our partners seldom follow our orders or do what we want them to do. Our partners just think what they think, say what they say, and do what they do — and they seldom change no matter how hard we try to get them to change.

The other day it struck me that this is in fact a really good thing. Because who would your partner be if you got things your way?

Who would your partner be if you — like some kind of God — were allowed to control the Universe and dictate how your partner should think, talk, act and live his or her life? For sure your partner wouldn't be the person he or she is right now, right? If you think about it, your partner wouldn't even be a person at all but rather a brain-dead slobbering robot sitting in the corner with saliva dribbling out of the corner of his mouth, waiting for your next command. "Yes, master, what is your command, master…?"

If you turn it around… who would you be if your partner got his way when it comes to you?

Who would you be if your partner — like some kind of God — could dictate and decide what you should think, say and do? It's a terrible thought, isn't it? You wouldn't be yourself any more but more like a vegetable or a tamed animal in a golden cage, just sitting there with a chain around your neck and shackles on your feet while you were told what to do.

Ugh, what a thought!

That's why the fact that we have absolutely no control over each other — no control over our partners or the other people in our lives — is such a good and wonderful thing. God couldn't have created anything more perfect. In fact, that's exactly how God did create it!

RELATIONSHIP MYTHS

My partner should/shouldn't _____.

I would be happy if my partner _____.

I know what is best for my partner.

Club "Shouldsville" —
the hottest club in town!

Have you heard of Club "Shouldsville"? Not only is Club "Shouldsville" (quite literally) the hottest place in town, it's a very special place—a lounge the Devil himself has reserved for the unhappiest VIP members in relationship hell. The entrance requirements for the club are actually quite straightforward. To become a VIP member of Club Shouldsville, you must constantly suffer from the belief that one "should" and "should not" say and do certain things in relationships. Since reality almost never lives up to most people's expectations and ideas about how their partners and their relationships "should" or "shouldn't" be, there are actually quite a lot of people who easily meet the entrance requirements of Club Shouldsville. Once admitted, Club Shouldsville is the place where all the "shouldists" can stamp and scream and wail and whine over the fact that their partners and their relationships are simply not living up to their ideas of what they think they "should" be.

So, you can see Club Shouldsville is a truly hellish corner of relationship hell. It's either sizzling like a furnace (for those who are frustrated or furious at their partners) or freezing cold (for those who love giving their partners the silent treatment and icy stares or sarcastic remarks that sting like hell). The interior design of the Club is pretty radical too. In one corner of the VIP club, there are stacks of broken dishes for people who need to vent their rage at their impossible partners. For the most extreme members, there is the "Blood & Gore" corner, with dolls that members can smash and trash and beat up all they want. Of course, there's also the trendiest bar in town, with everything the heart desires when it comes to booze, pills, smokes, and drugs for all the unhappy souls who want to drown their sorrow, pain and anger.

Another important entrance requirement to Club Shouldsville is that potential members do not know the difference between "I want", "I have to" and "I should". People who qualify for membership tend to mix the three together. Members of the club simply do not understand that "I want" is a free choice that often leads to "I have to". Here's a simple example of what club members fail to understand. Let's say "I want" to earn enough money every month so I can pay the rent and go to the movies once in a while. If that's the case, then "I have to" do something to earn the money—like going to work every day from nine to five. But there are no "shoulds" involved here. It doesn't say anywhere that "I should" or "shouldn't" have money enough to pay my rent and go to the movies. There's no law that says this. It's something I choose to do because "I want" to have enough money every month for my rent and the occasional movie.

In reality, the same holds true in relationships. There are no "shoulds" when it comes to relationships either. For example, when my girlfriend asks me to go with her to her family get-together this weekend, I can go or not go. There are no "shoulds" involved. But if my girlfriend tells me my going is a requirement if I want to be in a relationship with her—well, then, I have to make up my mind whether I want to or not. In other words, I have to decide if I am willing to pay the price for having her as my girlfriend. If going to the family event is the price and "I want" her to be my girlfriend, then "I have to" go. It's that simple. It's a straightforward exchange. But there are no "shoulds" involved—even if my girlfriend or I believe otherwise. Even if we believe that this is something one "should" do if one is a decent human being, if one really loves someone, or some other similar story. But in reality, there are no "shoulds" involved.

The problem is, members of Club Shouldsville seem to lack the ability to look at life in this realistic manner. They simply can't do it. Unfortunately, their inner myth-busting antenna is busted so they can't see the difference between reality and their thoughts and beliefs about what one "should" and "shouldn't" do in a relationship. Instead, they believe their thoughts with the same dedication and passion as the most die-hard fundamentalists. Anyone who questions their "shoulds" is threatened with eternal damnation in relationship hell.

But of course it doesn't work like that.

The only ones who go straight to relationship hell are the "shouldists" themselves, where they can hang out permanently, torturing themselves around the clock.

Right now, Club Shouldsville is opening its doors for a new wave of VIP members. Do you know any potential candidates? Or what about you?

RELATIONSHIP MYTHS
When one is in a relationship one should/shouldn't _____.
My partner should/shouldn't _____.
I should/shouldn't _____.

Who needs "commitment" when you have reality?

Sometimes people who read my questioning of our collective relationship myths ask me: "But Tim, what about 'commitment'? What about making promises and keeping them? What about having agreements and plans for the future?"

When people say this, what comes to mind is: "Who needs 'commitment' when you have reality?"

Just think about it for a moment and tell me honestly — how likely is it that you and your beloved are going to stop being together if you're a really good match, best friends, talk constantly about everything and just love hanging out with each other?

Not very likely, right?

Conversely, how likely is it that you and your partner — even though you're 'committed' to being together until death do you part — will stay together forever if you're bored to death in each other's company, can't really talk about what's important, and in fact can't stand each other?

Not very likely, right?

"But," you may say, "does this mean that two people can't promise each other that they'll stay together for the rest of their lives and never ever be together with anyone else? Does this mean that they can't do all this promising in a special building called the House of God with one of them dressed in a long, white gown while the other wears a black tuxedo and both are overseen by a third person in a white collar who reads solemn-sounding words from a book that is several thousand years old while their family and friends stand by and watch?"

Of course, the answer is you can! But if we get a tiny bit real about it all, we have to admit that it's just a tad absurd because everyone in this great building (including the solemn person in the white collar with the big book that is several thousand years old) knows perfectly well what the reality is: Namely that regardless of what these two people solemnly swear, they will stay together until they no longer stay together!

That's reality.

That reality may be a month, a year, or even ten years. Or even the rest of their lives. But standing there in the House of God, nobody knows for sure. Again, that's reality.

In one sense, having a wedding is just as absurd as if you and your best friend throw a big party and invite everyone you know and then solemnly swear in front of the whole crowd that the two of you will continue being best friends until death do you part! It would probably be a great party, but as for the rest...

"But," you may object, "Doesn't 'commitment' reduce the chances of one of the partners being unfaithful and being with someone else?"

Again, what comes to mind is: "Who needs 'commitment' when you have reality?"

If you and your partner really are the best friends in the whole wide world and can talk about everything and really love each other's company, what are the chances that one of you will be with someone else?

Pretty slim, right?

Conversely, if you and your partner are bored with each other and can't really be honest about what you feel—and maybe in the end can't stand the sight of each other—what are the chances that one of you (even though you swore fidelity in a church or town hall) will at some point be with someone else?

Pretty big, right?

This brings us to another good old myth about relationships which is: *My idea about what should happen in my life and in my relationship is better than what actually does happen.* It's the belief that *It would be better for me if my partner wasn't together with someone else.* The belief that *It would be better for me if my partner didn't leave me.* The belief that *It would be best for me if my partner and I stayed together forever.*

But when you think about the above statements, can you really know for sure that any of these statements are true? Can you really know what's best for you and your partner now or in the long run? Can you absolutely know that it's not the very best thing in the world for you (and for your partner) that your relationship ends when it ends? Which might be right now or next week?

Try to think back to a relationship you once had that didn't end the way you thought it should have. Then see if you can't quietly find at least three concrete reasons why your life is better today because that relationship ended when it did. At least three concrete reasons.

Now isn't that interesting?

So, can you absolutely know for sure that your idea about what should happen in your life—and in your relationship—is better than what is really happening?

As I said: Who needs 'commitment' when you have reality?

"But what about when you have children?" you may ask. "Doesn't that take 'commitment'?"

To this I'd say: Hey, what are the chances of you walking out the door and never returning if your one-year old baby is hungry and crying—whether or not you have a partner?

Pretty much zero, right?

So who needs 'commitment' when you have reality?

"But what about making plans and having agreements? If nobody knows what's going to happen in the future and reality always wins, does that mean that you can't make plans? I mean, can't we make plans to go out for dinner on Friday at seven, or to go on a holiday to the Maldives in January, or to buy a house or have a child together or …?"

The answer is yes, of course you can. Agreements and plans—such as making an appointment to get your hair done at three o'clock on Tuesday—are not something we do to make life more difficult for each other, but to make things easier. But the point is that no matter how many plans and agreements we make, the reality is that nobody knows what is going to happen tomorrow or next week or next year. We don't even know what's going to happen five seconds from now.

That's reality.

But there's nothing wrong with making plans and agreements. The problem arises when we stubbornly and rigidly hold on to these plans and agreements instead of living in harmony with the ever-changing and unpredictable reality. That's when we get into trouble and suffer. Especially if we're so attached to our plans for the future that we completely forget to live and enjoy the only thing we ever really have, which, when it comes to our relationship, is the two of us together in this moment. Now. Now. Now.

The fear of abandonment

If reading the above makes you feel upset or if you feel discomfort when you contemplate the fact that things really *do* change and that you don't need commitment when you have reality, it may be a sign that you have deeper issues. It may be a sign that you have an underlying fear of abandonment or that you are afraid of being alone or that you fear not being able to manage or take care of yourself if you are alone. Fears like these are common and are also based on some basic misunderstandings about the nature of life. In several of the coming chapters and in Part Two of this book, I investigate some of these fears and suggest ways in which you can learn to take better care of yourself—whether or not you have a partner.

RELATIONSHIP MYTHS

"Commitment" (such as marriage) increases the likelihood that my partner and I will stay together.

"Commitment" (such as marriage) reduces the likelihood that one of the partners will be unfaithful.

I know what is best for my partner.

I know what is best for me.

It would be best if my partner is not together with someone else.

It would be best if my partner does not leave me.

It would be best if I don't leave my partner.

Things shouldn't change.

You can't love more than one person at a time.

If my partner loves someone else, it means there's less love for me.

If I love someone else, it means there's less love for my partner.

Is a relationship only a success if it lasts until "death do us part"?

One day I was sitting with a client, helping her investigate her thoughts about her ex-husband. She and her ex had divorced some years earlier and ever since then, she'd felt that their relationship (they'd been married for ten years and had three lovely kids) had been a failure.

I asked her why she thought their relationship had been a failure and she looked at me as if I was really dense. Obviously, she said, because it ended.

When I asked her if she felt the same about the relationships she had before her marriage, she said that yes, they too had been failures. Because, she said, if a relationship ends, it must be a sign that it wasn't successful. My client believed that a relationship was only a success if it lasts until "death do us part".

Of course, she's not alone when it comes to this belief. As a matter of fact, most of us believe this to a greater or lesser degree. This belief has some lovely sub-beliefs such as: "The longer a relationship lasts, the better" and "People who are in one long-term relationship are happier than people who have been in several shorter relationships."

These interesting beliefs, which so many of us have, can lead to some pretty unhappy consequences. For those like my client, who are in a relationship that ends at some point, this belief often results in feeling the relationship was a failure. For others, this belief can make them stay in an unhappy relationship or marriage despite the fact that the people have grown apart and the relationship is no longer working.

But is this strong collective belief about relationships true? Does it have anything to do with reality when it comes to men and women? How did this belief arise in the first place?

One of the main reasons for the belief that a relationship is a failure if it ends (whether it's after three months, three years or thirty years) is probably because very few couples break up when things are going really well in their relationship. Most couples part ways when the relationship is no longer working or when people have grown apart. You rarely hear someone say that his or her relationship ended because: "Things were just going so well—you know we were best friends and had a great sex life—so we decided to break up!" No, that's not the way it works for most people!

So it's not hard to understand how many of us get the idea that a relationship that has ended is a failure. This is also because we tend to remember the end times of the relationship when things were no longer working and forget the many months or years when we shared good times together.

Another powerful reason why this belief has arisen can be found in the words of our Christian marriage vows:

> *"Do you _____ take _____ to be your lawfully wedded Wife/ Husband, to have and to hold from this day forward, for better for worse, for richer for poorer, in sickness and in health, to love and to cherish, till death do you part..."*

But just how much do these words have to do with the reality of life in the 21st century and with modern-day relationships?

Let's compare the reality of women and men today with the time when this marriage vow arose. (The precise date of origin of this widely used marriage vow is not known, but sources indicate that it dates back to the Apostle Paul's idea of men and women almost 2,000 years ago!)

- When you investigate a little more, you discover that this wedding vow comes from a time when women had no freedom or independence at all and were more or less just a piece of merchandise for men. The marriage ceremony merely sealed a business transaction between men. "I'll give you ten oxen and eighty chickens for your second daughter". The words "till death do you part" were just another way of saying that the woman was now the property of the new man until her death (and there was no such thing as "divorce" back then!).

- In contrast, women today (at least in the Western world) have as much freedom as men to live and create their own lives. They can decide who they want to be in a relationship with and they can leave a relationship if it is not satisfactory to them.

- When this wedding vow was born, the average life span was also a lot shorter than it is today. So, for a couple to be together "till death do you part" back then was not as long as it is for couples today! Today, with our improved living standard, "till death do you part" can be a very long time indeed!

~ Another important difference between then and now is that because of our longer life span, men and women today typically go through several "incarnations" during the course of one life. Not only do many of us have several jobs or even careers during one lifetime, many of us are also evolving very quickly on the inner plane. It's as if we go through several phases or "lives" in just one lifetime. So why shouldn't it be the same when it comes to relationships?

As you can see, there is a world of difference between the reality of life today and the way society operated when this marriage vow was born.

How would we feel if we lived more in harmony with reality when it comes to our changing relationships?

How would you feel if you viewed your relationships in the same way you probably view your career? When you think of your career, you probably feel it's pretty normal to go through various phases and periods—with changing workplaces and colleagues. When you start a new career path, you don't necessarily feel the old career path was a failure, you probably just feel you've grown and changed course and now want to try something new.

So, how would you feel if you viewed a relationship that ended in the same way? If you viewed it as a sign that you had received the gifts and lessons you were supposed to receive from this experience and were now ready to pass on to something new, something different, and maybe something even better? In other words, if you saw a relationship as complete when it was over, as a success for being exactly what it was for you—instead of as a failure just because it ended?

RELATIONSHIP MYTHS
A relationship is only a success if it lasts until death do us part.
The longer a relationship lasts, the better.
It's better to be in one long-term relationship than to be in several shorter relationships.

Are you in a relationship that's not good for you?

Are you in a relationship that doesn't support you and your life and who you really are? A relationship that drains you instead of uplifting you? One that is more destructive than constructive? More unhealthy than healthy? Have you tried everything you could think of to improve the situation and come to the conclusion that you and your partner are just not a good match? Have you discovered that you are not walking down the same path and that your core values don't match even though you may actually love each other?

Or are you in a relationship where your partner is aggressive, abusive and violates your boundaries — either verbally and/or physically?

If you are in a relationship that is not good for you, a relationship that is tearing you apart instead of nurturing and supporting you, the big question is: Why? Why do you stay in something that's not good for you? What are the reasons? What are the thoughts and beliefs that make you stay?

If you take a closer look at why you stay, you'll probably discover that your reasons fit into one or more of the following three categories:

1) **Fear of practical consequences**
2) **Beliefs**
3) **Attachment Hunger**

Let's take a closer look at each of these aspects:

1) FEAR OF PRACTICAL CONSEQUENCES

The fear of the practical consequences of ending a relationship is often the easiest to spot. Depending on how many things two people share (such as finances, home, children, friends, family, social life and how long they've shared them), ending a relationship will probably mean some far-reaching changes for their lives. If, for example, a woman has been a housewife who has stayed home, taking care of the kids while her husband worked, the end of the relationship will obviously entail some big changes that both parties must tackle. Perhaps the woman doesn't know how she will manage financially on her own. Maybe she has to adjust to the idea of being poorer and/or consider going back to work again. There can be worries about how the children will react to mom and dad splitting up, plus questions about custody, and how it will be to be a single mom or weekend dad. There may be questions about who is going to move out of their joint home and what that will mean. If they have the same friends and social circles, how will ending the relationship affect that? Yes, there is little doubt that ending a relationship can have far-reaching practical consequences that one or both partners may fear and that can be challenging or difficult to deal with.

If this is the case, it is a good idea to take the time to think through the consequences and take sensible steps to prepare for the changes. For some people, a support team of friends and family can help provide guidance and support through these changes.

In addition to considering and preparing for the practical consequences, it can also be a good idea to take a closer look at the thoughts and stories you have about these consequences. Investigate whether the stories about what you fear are as true as you may believe.

You may for example believe thoughts like:

> *I won't be able to manage on my own financially.*
> *I'm too old to start working again.*
> *I don't know how to start a new career.*
> *It's too late to upgrade my skills.*
> *The children won't be able to handle their parents splitting up.*
> *I'll lose all my friends.*

Or any such similar thoughts…

If you are struggling with thoughts like the above (which may also be keeping you in an unhappy relationship), write them down on a piece of paper and then turn to Part Two of this book to learn how to investigate these troubling thoughts.

It can be a great help to look carefully at these thoughts to discover the truth of your situation. Because can you absolutely know for sure that it will be as difficult to manage on your own as you may fear? Can you absolutely know that you can't manage? If you're worried about your children, can you absolutely know what's best for your children in the long run? (Is it better for them to have a mother and father who are together but constantly arguing?) If you investigate your troubling thoughts, you may discover that you cannot be absolutely sure that the practical consequences will be as terrible or as insurmountable as you may fear. You may also discover you have more resources than you were aware of. Perhaps you will discover there is help to be found in places and from people you have not considered before.

I'm not saying that the practical consequences will necessarily be easy, but I would like to suggest that you investigate whether or not the practical consequences will be as difficult and insurmountable as you may fear.

2) BELIEFS

In addition to the fear of the practical consequences of ending a relationship, there are also many other thoughts and beliefs that can make a person stay in an unhappy relationship. They can be collective social beliefs such as:

Love conquers all.
We promised before God to stay together till death do us part,
    so we should stay together no matter what.
A relationship is only a success if it lasts until death do us part.
I'm a failure if this relationship ends.
We really love each other, so we should be able to make it work.
Sooner or later, he/she will change.
We're just going through a rough period.
I shouldn't be so selfish.
Sometimes you just have to bite the bullet.
I should stay and try to make it work.

Or it may be thoughts about what it will mean for your partner:

My partner will be devastated if I leave him/her.
My partner won't be able to manage without me.

It may also be the fear of being alone. For example:

I'll be so lonely.
I can't manage on my own.

I'll never find a new partner.
I'm too old to find a new partner.
I'm no longer that attractive; no one will want me.

If some of these beliefs are causing you to stay in an unhappy relationship, again it's a good idea to write them down and investigate them using one of the techniques described in Part Two.

Let's look at a few of these for a moment. So is it true that because two people love each other, they should also be able to make their relationship work? You and your partner probably do love each other or at least did at some point. But does this mean that at this point in your lives, you both want the same things and still have matching values and preferences? Not necessarily, because the reality is that everyone is evolving and people do change. So perhaps you've simply grown in different directions.

If it's the fear of being alone, you can also take a closer look at these thoughts and see if they have anything to do with reality. Can you absolutely know that you will be all alone for the rest of your life if this relationship ends? (By the way, what's wrong with being alone for a while anyway?) Can you know for sure that you won't meet new and exciting people who may be a lot more in harmony with who you are today and who it will be a lot healthier for you to hang out with? Can you absolutely know that you won't meet a new partner who will be a much better match for who you are today and what you want now? Finally, can you absolutely know what is best for you and your partner in the long run?

3) ATTACHMENT HUNGER

The third reason people stay in unhappy or dysfunctional relationships is often the most difficult to understand—both for the people in the relationship and for people looking in from the outside. The reason, which the psychologist Howard M. Halpern calls "Attachment Hunger", is actually a form of addiction. According to Halpern, it's an addiction that stems from a deep, fundamental longing to experience love, oneness and a sense of safety combined with the almost hypnotic belief that it is only possible to experience this love and oneness with one particular partner (even though the relationship may be deeply unhappy and unhealthy for both partners). (For more about this mechanism, see Halpern's book *How to Break Your Addiction to a Person*.)

According to Halpern, "Attachment Hunger" has its roots in the early stages of life when as an infant we experienced a powerful sense of oneness, safety and love with our mother. This sense of oneness gradually ends as the infant grows and the mother and child slowly begin to separate, with the support of a good father. But according to Halpern, if this separation does not happen gradually in a smooth and healthy way, then many people will continue as adults to try to recreate and re-experience in their adult relationships the ecstatic feeling of oneness, safety and love they experienced in infancy and then lost.

This is not necessarily a problem, especially if the partners are a good match. But it can be problematic when this powerful longing makes a person stay in a relationship that is unhealthy, abusive or perhaps even violent. To someone watching from the outside who does not understand the power of "Attachment Hunger" and the addiction to an unhealthy relationship that it causes, a relationship like this may seem completely incomprehensible. How can someone who seems otherwise reasonably sane and sensible stay in such a dysfunctional relationship? Yes, it's complicated and obviously this is only a very brief introduction to a very multi-faceted subject. But if this rings a bell with you, I highly recommend reading Halpern's book for a better understanding of "Attachment Hunger" and its distressing consequences.

In brief, I will however say that if you're suffering from "Attachment Hunger" and it makes you stay in a dysfunctional relationship, or if you have left your partner and feel an overwhelming desire to return against your better judgment, there are several things you can work on right away:

A) **Remind yourself of the difference between your infantile longing and your wisdom**

When you are in the throes of "Attachment Hunger", it is absolutely essential to remind yourself that this powerful, at times almost overwhelming sense of attraction and longing to be with the other person, does not come from your wisdom. It has its origins in an infantile longing to recreate the sense of oneness and love you feel you have lost. Just being aware of this can be a tremendous help when it comes to breaking free of an unhealthy relationship. (It can also help you steer clear of entering another unhealthy one!). The more aware you become of this mechanism, the easier it will be for you to let your choices and actions be guided by your adult wisdom — and not by your infantile longings.

B) **Make a "negative" list**

If you have just left someone or are thinking about leaving someone and "Attachment Hunger" is tearing you apart, it can help to remind yourself of the unhealthy and destructive consequences of staying in a dysfunctional relationship that does not harmonize with your adult wisdom and sanity but is driven by "Attachment Hunger".

So before you succumb to an attack of longing for this person, make a list of all the unhealthy and destructive consequences this relationship has for you and your life. Write it all down. For example:

- This relationship is wearing me down mentally, emotionally and physically.
- The endless conflicts and disagreements we have are using up an enormous amount of my time and energy.
- This drain on my time and energy makes me neglect other important and enjoyable areas of my life, such as my family and friends.
- Because of this relationship, I neglect my creative projects, because all the worrying and quarreling block my creativity.
- I could make better use of the time I spend worrying about this relationship. I could, for example, meet new, stimulating people who are supportive and healthy for me instead.
- This enormous drain on my time and energy has a detrimental effect on my performance at work. So it is affecting my career and my finances.
- I have trouble sleeping.
- I eat too much.
- I drink too much.
- I don't have time to exercise.
- The stress is affecting my health.
- I've lost my peace of mind.
- I'm a nervous wreck because of this relationship.
  And so on.

So yes, there is little doubt that a relationship run by "Attachment Hunger" can really mess up a person's life in the same way the addictive behavior of an alcoholic or drug addict can gradually destroy a person's life. An unhealthy addiction to a person can be just as serious and dangerous.

So when the longing to be with the other person feels almost irresistible, bring out your "negative" list and spend some time understanding what all this means for your life and happiness. This practice can quickly help you get "sober" again!

C) **Find healthy love in other places**

Since "Attachment Hunger" originates in a longing to experience a sense of oneness, safety and love, it is important to find and cultivate more healthy ways to experience these feelings. You can, for example, focus on experiencing oneness and love by spending time in nature and feeling your oneness with Mother Earth, the Universe and a Higher Power. Or you can focus on experiencing oneness and love by helping others, doing community service and working for the welfare of humanity. You can also focus on the oneness and love that you experience when you are with your family and friends. Or spend more time playing with children (and practice giving lots of loving hugs!). You can also paint, sing, dance, write or enjoy some other kind of creative activity. Or start a business, walk from Norway to Spain or take up mountain climbing. Or you can try to cultivate this love and oneness by working on having a more loving and harmonious relationship with yourself (more about this in the following chapters). You can also spend more time focusing on your own personal development or develop a spiritual practice or go to therapy or join a 12-step group. There are many excellent, healthy ways of experiencing the love that you are longing for.

RELATIONSHIP MYTHS

The love that I seek is dependent on another person.
I can only experience the love that I seek with one special person.

Be the partner you seek

Many years ago I went to a lecture with the Indian master Sri Sri Ravi Shankar. One of the people at the talk was unhappy because he didn't have a partner and he asked Ravi Shankar what he could do to get a partner. Ravi Shankar laughed and said: "The reason why you are looking for a partner is because you are so bored in your own company. And if you're bored in your own company, just think how bored other people must be when they are with you!"

Master Shankar had a good point there. We are often so focused on getting what we want—good company, fun, warmth, love, support, friendship—from a partner that we completely forget that twenty-four hours a day, seven days of the week, each of us always has someone by our side that can give us all the things we want a partner to give us.

Namely ourselves!

If we don't give ourselves the things we want a partner to give us, if we ourselves are not the loving, fun, inspiring, supportive, friendly person we hope our partner will be, why on earth would another human being be interested in hanging out with us!?

This is why it's a good idea (as Ravi Shankar said to this man) to start giving yourself what you want a partner to give you and to work on being the wonderful person that you want a partner to be for you. One of the ways you can do this is by making a list of the things you want a partner to be and do for you. For example, *I want a partner who (or I want my partner to):*

Love me unconditionally
Support me
Understand me
Be interested in what I do
Be fun and adventurous
Be loving and kind
Be a good friend
Take care of me and protect me
Be totally honest with me
And so forth.

Then be the partner you seek. Give yourself what you want a partner or your partner to give you:

Love yourself unconditionally
Support yourself
Understand yourself
Be interested in what you do
Be fun and adventurous
Be loving and kind
Be a good friend to yourself
Take care of yourself and protect yourself
Be totally honest with yourself
And so forth.

Can you do that? As you may discover, it's easier said than done! But on the other hand, if you can't do it, why would another person be interested in or even capable of doing this? Just think about it — we're talking about another person who doesn't even remotely have the same qualifications as you to know what you think, feel and want!

Fortunately for us, life is designed in such a way that each one of us has all the necessary qualifications to give ourselves precisely and exactly what we want another person to give us! It's really very simple because no one knows more about us than we do. Nobody knows better than you what kind of music you like. Nobody knows better than you what you like having for breakfast. Nobody knows better than you what you have been through in your life. Nobody knows better than you what you need right now. So why not give it to yourself?

It's also a good idea when you're with other people to work on being the kind of person or partner you want other people or your partner to be towards you. If you want your partner to be honest, then you be honest with your partner and the people in your life. If you want your partner to understand you, then you try to understand your partner and the people in your life.

In other words, be the partner you seek!

RELATIONSHIP MYTH
I need a partner to be happy.

How is your "relationship" with yourself?

The only relationship that lasts your whole life and can never end is the relationship you have with yourself. Just think about it. It's so obvious that many of us don't notice it. No matter who you are, no matter what you do, no matter where you are, no matter what time of day it is, you're always with you! No matter how hard you try, you can't get rid of yourself! That's why sometimes, like when I'm travelling, I find myself laughing and saying to myself: "Wherever I go—there I am!"

The relationship you have with yourself is the only relationship you're in that lasts your whole life. One could say you're married to yourself and it's not possible to get a divorce! You always go to bed with you and you always wake up with you. Whether you are alone or with other people, you're always with you.

You, you, you!

But just how good is your relationship with yourself?

If you looked at your relationship with yourself in the same way you look at your relationship with someone else—like with a partner or a good friend—well, just how good would you say your relationship with yourself is? Do you enjoy your own company? Are you a good friend to yourself? Do you love and accept yourself the way you probably hope a partner or a good friend will love and accept you?

Do you support yourself and respect yourself the way you probably want other people to support and respect you? Do you understand yourself and your thoughts and emotions? Do you understand and sympathize with the life you've had and the life you're having right now? How understanding are you when it comes to the challenges you are facing at the moment? Are you as faithful to yourself, your heart and dreams as you would probably want your partner to be towards you and your dreams? Can you honestly say to yourself that you will *have and hold yourself...for better for worse, for richer for poorer, in sickness and in health...that you will love and cherish yourself...*" for the rest of your life?

So how good is your relationship with yourself?

A good way to find out is to regularly spend some time alone with yourself in silence. All by yourself, in the silence. With no activity or talking. With no radio, music, books, magazines, television or computer to distract you. Just the two of you. You with you. Sitting in a chair, doing nothing. Just looking and feeling. In the silence. This moment. Who are you? What are your thoughts? How do you feel? How are you? Take the time to notice. Take the time to really be with you.

If you don't like being alone with yourself, why should anyone else?

If you don't have a good relationship with the person you are closer to than anyone else in life, the person you are always with, how can you have a good relationship with other people? If you don't have a loving, accepting, supportive and understanding relationship with yourself, how can you have a loving, accepting, supportive and understanding relationship with other people? Or them with you? It simply can't be done. Because the relationship you have with yourself—for better or for worse—is also the relationship you have with other people. The relationship you have with other people—for better or for worse—is also the relationship you have with yourself.

totalorgasmicbliss

The most powerful experience of love I've ever had occurred some years ago while I was on a beach in Tel Aviv, Israel. I like to call what I experienced that day "totalorgasmicbliss". It was early April and springtime in God's Own Country, so the temperature was fine and there was a gentle breeze coming from the ocean. I was sitting on the sand about 10-15 meters from the water's edge and a good distance away from the Banana Beach café's merry reggae music. (I'd been in Israel several times that year and discovered that the beach cafés had tape loops playing the same music over and over again, every single day). It must have been around noon when I decided to try sitting still and doing nothing for a couple of hours. Sitting quietly doing nothing for an hour or so was something I'd "done" before, but for some reason, on that day I decided to try doing it for much longer — like for several hours!

When I say "doing nothing" I mean:

1) Not doing anything at all. Not engaging in any "activities" like reading or eating or doing anything. I mean just sitting quietly with my eyes open and looking straight ahead — at whatever is in front of me. In this case it was the sand and water. The waves lapping on the shore. The sun reflecting on the sea. People passing by. Me moving as little as possible. Changing positions once in a while — from sitting cross-legged to squatting to sitting with my legs stretched out to lying a little on my side. Whatever felt most comfortable.
2) Not talking to anybody or saying anything. Being completely quiet.
3) Not doing anything mentally, inside myself, in my head. By this, I do not mean that thoughts do not constantly arise and disappear again in my mind, because of course they do. Thoughts arise and disappear like they always do. What I do mean is not to engage in or attach to these thoughts. Or to be more precise — To try not to. In other words, every time I notice that I'm attaching to a thought, or becoming engrossed in one, I stop immediately and return to just sitting and observing and doing nothing.

4) Another important thing about "doing nothing" is I do not "meditate" in the traditional sense of the word. In other words, I don't focus on the breathing or on a mantra or on some other focus point. I just allow my mind to be completely free and don't try to direct it. I just let it do whatever it does. You could call this "non-meditation" meditation!

As soon as I began sitting still doing nothing, I had the usual reaction. This was something I'd experienced all the other times I'd tried to sit quietly and do nothing. It felt as if my thoughts simply went amok, really amok. Every thought that arose was a thought that was emphatically resisting what I was doing—or rather "not doing"!

Most of the thoughts were variations on the same basic theme and went something like this:

"This, this moment, what is right now, is not good enough."

"There's something better than this."

"There's something better somewhere in the future, in some other place than here."

"Something is missing."

"You'd be happier if you were doing something else."

"You have to do something (to attain some state that is 'better' than this state)."

"This is a complete waste of time."

"This is not leading anywhere."

"You should be doing something productive."

"You should be trying to achieve something."

… and so on.

It felt as if these thoughts were pulling and pushing me from all sides like the arms of a giant who was trying to yank me away from sitting there totally "wasting" my time doing nothing. According to these thoughts, there were so many other important things to do—somewhere in the future at some place other than right here. Yes my thoughts literally went nuts over this colossal, meaningless "waste" of important time! Time that I could have spent so much more profitably, doing something, achieving something, which would make me happier and more complete than I was at that moment (again according to my thoughts). But no matter how vociferously the thoughts inside me raged and howled and protested, I just kept sitting quietly with my eyes open, staring into space doing nothing.

Once in a while, when one of these really noisy, painful thoughts kept arising and arising and I could see that I was really attached to it, I silently investigated the thought in my head using the four questions of The Work of Byron Katie. (For more about how to do this, see page 149).

So that day on the beach by Tel Aviv, I started by investigating the mother of all stressful thoughts—namely:

"*There's something better than this.*"

In my head I asked myself the first question of The Work of Byron Katie:

Is it true?

Is it true that there's something better than this?

Yes. I think so.

Then I silently asked myself the second question:

Can you absolutely know that it's true that there's something better than this? Can you absolutely know that there is something better than what is in this moment, better than what is right now?

Can you absolutely know that there is anything other than what is in this moment? In fact, is there anything other than this moment? Is it even possible to experience anything other than this moment? And if there's nothing else but this moment, if there is no time, if there is no past or future, if there is no movement at all, if you don't move at all, then how can there be *something better than this*? If there's nothing other than this moment, this now, this, how can there be something better?

So…*Can you absolutely know that there's something better than this?*

Pause.

Silence.

No, I can't know that.

Wow.

I really can't know that for sure.

Interesting…

I moved on to question number three:

How do you react when you believe the thought that there's something better than this, something better than what is right now?

My silent answer was: Well, then I try to get away from the now, from this, from what is right here, right now. I'm at war with the now; I'm at war with myself, with everything, with life itself. It makes me feel discomfort. I feel uncomfortable about myself, about my body, about where I am. This resistance is hell. I have all these thoughts about what it takes to make life better than this, about what outer circumstances I need to make life better than this, and I spend my entire life, all my waking hours, trying to attain this. It's always disappearing, fleeting. Always just around the corner, always at the end of the nearest rainbow. Always out there, somewhere else, other than right here. And then what happens? Well then I miss the only thing I ever have, which is this. This moment. This now. It's as if I'm sick, feverish, and it makes me feel anxious and uncomfortable with life. It's so stressful that I can't be fully present anywhere. I'm always on my way somewhere else. This makes it really difficult, almost impossible, to sit here. It's awful!

When I believe this thought I also feel insecure about myself when I'm with other people. I feel insecure about myself even when I'm just with me, all alone. It's pure hell. It's really stressful ... stress, stress, stress. No matter how hard I try, I can't think of a single reason to keep this thought that does not feel stressful. Because this thought *is* stress!

This thought—the thought that *there's something better than this*—is the mother of all my stress!

From this thought, other stressful thoughts arise, such as: This is not good enough," "It would be better if…," "I would be happier if…." "Something is missing." "I'm incomplete the way I am." "I need to do something…," "I need to achieve something."

Now on to the fourth question:

Who would you be without the thought that there's something better than this?

Aaaaaaaaaahhhhh! I would be like a balloon when you let the hot air out! All the tension, all the effort, all the resistance that makes me so tense and stresses me day and night would be gone, just like that, and I would let go completely. Like when you have a really good orgasm and everything inside you just stops. Just completely stops. There's no more fighting or resisting or tension or trying or doing or achieving or anything. You just go limp, your whole body, every muscle—your mind, your thoughts, your emotions, your heart... Oh, yes, the heart... It would be like a pure orgasm of the heart. I would be like a golden flowing river of light, an ocean of aaahhhh. It would be over. It would be the end, the end of the endless struggle. The end of all that effort and I would be done. Finished. Over. Then, I would no longer believe in or act on all the absurd thoughts that say I would be happier, more OK, feel better, if I achieved this or that. No, it would be over. I would be over. There would be peace. *I would be peace.*

Finally, the last part of The Work of Byron Katie: the turnaround. So, I turned the original thought around to its complete opposite, and this is what I got:

There's nothing better than this.

Could that be as true or truer?

Pause.

Silence.

Yes!

Yes indeed!

There's nothing better than this. Because the fact is, there is nothing other than this! There's never been anything other than this. Me (or whatever "I" am) sitting here, unmoving, watching all these fascinating movies and stories pass by (with eyes opened or closed). The fascinating story of Tim flying in from his home far, far away to visit his Israeli girlfriend in this strange and exotic world…The fascinating story of Tim in Tel Aviv, meeting an Israeli publisher… The fascinating story of this or that.

There's nothing better than this. Because no matter what happens in my life, I'm always here. It's all about me, it all comes from me and disappears back into me. Things can move and change around me (they constantly do), but I never change. I don't evolve. I remain the same.

There's nothing better than this. Because if God is All and God is Good (which, as far as I can see, is the way things are), then whatever is right now must be the very best. Yes exactly this—what is right now — must be the best. Heaven. If the very best is not right now, if I have to do something or achieve something or become worthy of the very best, then God cannot be Good. A God who would demand things like this cannot be Good because no God who is boundless, unlimited, unconditional Love would do something like that. God is Good. Of this I am certain.

There's nothing better than this. Yes. Because when I don't believe the stressful thought that *there's something better than this*, something that I should do or achieve, then *there's nothing better than this!*

I could also see another way to turn the original thought around.

There's something worse than this.

Yes.

My thinking! My thinking is much worse than this! The thought that *there's something better than this*, something I have to do or achieve to be happy and OK, is pure hell. My thoughts are much, much worse than this.

I could see yet another turnaround.

There's something better than my thinking.

Yes! This is better! This, whatever this is right now, is so much better than my thinking! Me just sitting here on the beach in heaven with nothing to do, nothing to achieve, forever perfect and OK. This is so much better than anything my thinking could ever concoct, not even in my wildest dreams!

After I investigated this thought, this core belief—the mother of all stressful thoughts—with the four questions, I continued sitting on the beach, staring at the sea. The minutes passed and again and again thoughts would arise and disappear. I was able to observe most of these thoughts as they arose and disappeared the way all thoughts do. But once in a while I'd realize I'd become really absorbed in a thought and was now mentally travelling in its universe, but every time I became aware of this, I would stop and return to sitting quietly doing nothing.

But still, thoughts did arise, which "bothered" me so much that I had difficulty not attaching to them. They were thoughts such as: "This is not good enough" or "You should be doing something". Each time this happened, I again quietly investigated the thought in my head with the four questions:

Is it true?

Can I absolutely know that it's true?

How do I react when I believe that thought?

Who would I be without the thought?

Turn the thought around.

Then I would return to just sitting quietly doing nothing.

After I'd been sitting quietly doing nothing for a while, it dawned on me that the reason I'd decided to do this in the first place was because I believed that if I could actually sit quietly and do nothing for several hours I'd feel better than I did before I started… In other words, I realized that my motivation for sitting quietly doing nothing was actually the thought *"There's something better than this"*!

When I realized this, I burst out laughing!

What a joke!

It was amazing to see!

Amazing how confused the mind can be! How confused my mind was!

In that moment, I really got it and I realized that some magical state that was better than this was simply not going to happen!

I realized that *this is it.*

This is the magical state.

This is as good as it gets.

Yes, this is it.

So, I continued sitting quietly, doing nothing. Again those stormy, rebellious thoughts would arise, yelling "You're wasting your time", "You have to do something", "There's something wrong with you", and more.

Still, I continued sitting quietly. And the hours went by.

In front of me, one scene after another played itself out. People passed by—couples, the young, the old, men, women, children… The world passed by along the water's edge. Two dogs ran merrily by and seemed to be enjoying themselves hugely. Then I noticed that one of the dogs had only three legs. I also noticed that this dog seemed to be just as happy and satisfied as the dog with four legs. The three-legged dog didn't have the story that four legs are better than three.

And I was just like the three-legged dog! I no longer believed that something was better than anything else—or that there was something that was better than this!

As the hours went by and I continued sitting there doing nothing, I began to feel well…yes…rather…peaceful. Actually, it's kind of hard to put into words what I actually felt. But yes, it was rather peaceful because I knew there was nothing wrong with me and that I didn't lack anything. I knew that this is it. That it couldn't get better than this. Ever. This was it. Plain and simple.

It was as if my mind was peace. It's not that my mind was peaceful but that my mind itself was peace. That was what I was—peace. Yes peace was what I was. Everything else, all the thoughts, emotions, the body and its sensations, the world, the beach, the people passing by, were just bubbles on the surface of this infinite ocean of peace that I was. Wow.

And I continued to sit there.

In fact, I felt that I could just sit there forever, that I would just sit there forever, while the stories and dreams of my life passed by, day after day. There was nothing but this moment, this now. There was literally no story of a past or a future. Or if they sometimes arose, they seemed so unreal, dreamlike. But now, here, as I try to write this… It's very difficult to put into words what I experienced then.

Still I sat there. The sun began to go down. The time was… I must have sat there quietly for at least four, five, maybe six hours. There was a golden light over the land. Shining on the sand, the beach, the people, everything. I literally felt as if I was an orgasm. As if I was pure bliss. Yes, it wasn't something that I experienced or felt (although I most certainly also experienced and felt it), it was what I was. *totalorgasmicbliss.* I felt so relaxed that I almost couldn't sit up so I just sort of surrendered myself to the sand the way you do when you have an orgasm. Ah! Ah! Ah! Right in the heart, in the mind. It all exploded and all the barriers, all the obstacles, every thought of past or future was gone. Simply vanished and there was only this. There was only Tim, lying in the sand gasping, smiling, in an orgasm with no end. It was as if my whole body, every cell and atom, was bliss, a golden river of bliss. Everything around me was golden bliss too. There was this amazing light that fell on everything — radiated from everything. Everything was so beautiful. I couldn't believe I hadn't noticed it before. Everything was bathed in such silence, such love, such tenderness, even the things that my mind before had categorized as being ugly or unfriendly …

It was as if everything was moving very slowly. Not slow in the sense that it was slower than before. But slow in the sense that it was "me" who was noticing for the very first time how everything really was. How incredibly beautiful everything really was, how amazing the indescribable heavenly gracefulness of everything was. How it all moved and flowed in one silent and amazing symphony of love — the cars, the houses, the people, the sounds, the sidewalk, the seagulls, the garbage cans, the dogs, the… ah ah ah…

It had always been like this. Always. It had always been… *This is it.* I just never noticed it before.

But now I did. Now I saw. Now it was over and I was home. Home where I'd always been. Home. There it was and I couldn't leave it. I was home. Home was me.

It was so simple — and the mind had made it all so complicated.

I felt that I could sit there forever. I would have loved to sit there forever. I looked to my left and noticed a woman sitting not far from me. She smiled at me. For a brief moment I thought of flirting. Yes the thought of flirting momentarily arose, skipping across the surface of my peace. And then it was gone. I saw how unimportant and small and insignificant all flirting was compared to this. I smiled at the thought and continued to smile — at everything and everyone. Then I looked back at the ocean and continued sitting quietly doing nothing.

Then I remembered I had an appointment that evening with an editor from an Israeli publishing house. We were supposed to meet at a café in the center of town. Slowly, it seemed very slowly, I took out my phone and checked the time. It would probably be a good idea to start walking over there now. I felt like laughing and felt curious — wondering how it would be to meet this editor when everything was moving so blissfully slow. So I got up. Again, it seemed as if everything was happening very slowly. Then I packed my things and began walking, slowly, step by step, across the warm golden sand towards the city.

And oh what a city it was! I'd never been so in love with a city before! In love with everything. It all seemed so indescribably wonderful… I remember walking across the hot concrete, across the hot square, the concrete baking in the setting sun, the square almost totally deserted, surrounded by low white buildings on all sides. It all seemed so delicious… so… like you could just eat it, like I could eat it… the smells, the sounds, all the sensory input, the colors … even the garbage and the crumpled cardboard boxes and the garbage cans, the rotten fruit, and the old trucks and the old trees, the run-down houses … Never before had anything been so clear, so alive, so beautiful, so near, so dear, so me, so … oh how I loved that square and everything in it and oh how I would have loved to keep on walking across that square and loving it all forever … But I kept on walking, slowly, like the silence itself, like the huge vast silence in which the entire world and all its colors and shapes was dancing … across the square … through Tel Aviv's busy Carmel market … Again I walked very slowly, allowing the glory of everything to penetrate me … The stalls, the fruit, the vegetables, the beautiful men, the beautiful women, the street vendors haggling over prices, the cavalcade of colors, an incredible, amazing universe, which I simply loved through and through. How wonderful! What splendor! What magnificence! Such an amazing abundance and all of it bathed in this loving golden light. A woman was walking towards me; it was the same woman who had been sitting to my left on the beach and who'd smiled at me. Now she smiled at me again. How funny! What a miracle! That the same beautiful woman (and oh I will never forget how beautiful she was) should pass me once again along with everything else that was passing by. I smiled and we both laughed, as if we both knew that yes, yes, this, this was nothing less than heaven.

I continued to walk down the streets and avenues of Tel Aviv, all bathed in this amazing golden light. The cars and the stores and the names of the streets with their fascinating Hebrew letters … I walked down a long boulevard. Now where was the café where I was supposed to meet this editor? Was it this street? Perhaps I should ask someone. So I asked a woman. She didn't know. But oh was she lovely. I walked on. Three young women were walking towards me. I asked them and was totally spellbound by their beauty and by the words that came out of their mouths. They were so helpful, asking me questions. Asking me where was I from. So much help and I almost hadn't said a word. I could have stood there and talked to them forever but hey, it turned out that the café was right there — just across the street! Thank you, goodbye, bless you, I love you.

Inside the café — and oh what a café it was — everything was splendid — the interior design, the chairs, the sound of soft music, the people at the bar. There was my friend, the editor. How groovy it was to see him there. A part of this, all of this. It was so exciting, such an adventure! You, me, this, like Arabian Nights on an ordinary Thursday evening in Tel Aviv! Anything could happen and anything was happening. He invites me up to the first floor so we can sit and talk without being disturbed. The owner of the café is a good friend of his; the café is the editor's favorite café. The owner is so friendly. What would I like.

I can have anything I want, amazing, drinks, coffee, tea, food, dessert; I feel like a prince, truly the royal treatment.

My friend the editor, he too is truly amazing. So beautiful! Incredible that I didn't notice it until now, the beautiful silver bracelet on his wrist, his dark curls, the way he smokes his cigarette; and it's so fascinating to hear him talk. It's much more fascinating to hear him talk than anything else I can think of. To hear everything he has to say about book releases and agents and author tours... He is so beautiful and everything is so beautiful that I find it difficult to take any of the things he is saying seriously. All these thoughts about the future that I once thought were so important—because how can anything in the future, how can any book release or author tour give me even a fraction more than all that I have right now, right this very moment, right here, right now in this café in Tel Aviv, at the very Heart of the Heart of the Universe... Yes, this is it.

What about the great love?

OR

The mother of all relationship myths

After reading some of my observations about our collective relationship myths, a female friend said to me, "You know everything you say sounds very sensible and true, Tim, but to be honest it makes me kind of sad. I mean what about the great love? Is that also just another myth or a silly belief? Because if it is, I think I'd rather live with the lie because life would simply be too empty and depressing without it …"

But as I said to my friend, the great love is not a myth. The myth is the belief that *the great love is outside us and dependent on another person.* Which is why I often call this myth "the mother of all relationship myths", simply because this is probably the greatest misunderstanding of all when it comes to love and relationships. When you start to notice, you discover it's a fantastic, all-consuming myth that is the theme of thousands and thousands of pop songs as well as the driving force behind huge commercial ventures, including TV series, books, magazines as well as the fashion and beauty industries.

The reason why I call the idea that the great love is outside us and dependent on another person a myth is because that's precisely what it is. An ancient myth, an old wives' tale, a fable, that has absolutely nothing to do with reality, the reality of men and women and relationships.

The reality is that love and the joy of being are not outside us. Love and the joy of being are inside us. This is because love and the joy of being are our nature; it is what we are. (For more about this, see the previous chapter "total-orgasmicbliss".) No one can add anything to the love and joy that you and I are. No one can take away the love and joy that you and I are.

But then why don't we always experience love?

"But if love and joy are really our nature," you might ask, "then why don't we (always) experience it? Why do we sometimes feel sad, anxious and lonely?" Why do we sometimes feel that life is empty and depressing?

The answer is simple: Since love and joy are our nature, something must be blocking the experience of this love since we don't always feel it. What is that? What is preventing us from experiencing our true nature, which is love?

If you look closely at the way the mind works, you will see that what is preventing us from experiencing our true nature is the whole range of thoughts we believe in that have nothing to do with reality. Thoughts and beliefs, which block the experience of love because these thoughts are unloving or the opposite of love. Thoughts and beliefs, which obscure our true nature. Thoughts and beliefs such as: "Life is dangerous", or "I need to be in control", or "If I don't take care, things won't go well", or "There's something wrong with me", or "I'm not good enough", or "I need _____ to be OK and happy", or "I need people to like me", and so on. As you can see, all of these thoughts are a far cry from love.

When we believe untrue thoughts and stories about ourselves and about life like the ones mentioned above, these thoughts are like clouds before the sun. They temporarily block the experience of the love and the joy of being that we are. It's not that the love that we are disappears (that's not possible), but we temporarily lose the awareness of it because we are so absorbed in these distressing thoughts. In other words, when we believe thoughts like these that is what we experience — instead of our true nature, which is love.

This is obviously very painful, so naturally we will do anything and everything we can to experience that love and the joy of being again. We'll even pass through fire and water to put an end to that terrible feeling of loss and experience that love again.

But because we're not aware of our true nature and not aware of the real cause of our pain and longing, we try to end our suffering in ways that are doomed to failure. So unfortunately for us, in our ignorance, we seek love and joy outside ourselves, in other people and in outer circumstances instead of seeking love where it really is — inside ourselves.

In our innocent confusion, the place where we most desperately seek this love and joy is in romantic relationships. Yes, we seek it in the story of "the one and only", in the story of "soul mates", in the dream of that one special man or woman who we think will give us the experience of the love and joy we seek. This story, this myth — that the love and joy of being that we seek is outside us

113

and dependent on another person—is one of the cornerstones of our confusion and unhappiness when it comes to relationships.

So how did this myth arise?

One reason we believe this myth is that many of us do actually experience love and the joy of being (or at least glimpses of it) when we are with our partners. Especially during the falling-in-love stage or when we're having great sex! This experience seems to prove that the myth is true. It seems to prove that the love that you seek really is dependent on finding this one special person and being with him or her. Because yes it's true, when we're with our beloved, many of us do seem to experience glimpses of love and joy. Sometimes even more than just glimpses; sometimes we're ecstatically happy.

But is the fact that we sometimes experience love and the joy of being when we are with our beloved really proof that the love and joy we are experiencing comes from this person or is dependent on this person? At first glance it sounds plausible, but is it really true?

This question is worth considering carefully.

So let's backtrack a moment. If—as I said before—the nature of reality is that you and I *are* love, then why don't we always experience this love? As I said, we don't always experience this love because we believe in stressful, unloving thoughts and stories that have nothing to do with reality and which actually "block" the experience of the love because we are so absorbed in these thoughts. When this happens, the love doesn't disappear but we temporarily lose our awareness of it. Just like when the clouds block the rays of the sun. The sun doesn't disappear; we just can't see it.

But—and now here comes the interesting part—our absorption in our thoughts and beliefs is not constant. Sometimes there are gaps. Sometimes there are moments when we're not so absorbed in our thinking. Then what happens? What happens is, bang, without the clouds, the sun is suddenly shining and we experience the love and joy that is our true nature. All of a sudden, it's just there. Just the way it happened to me that day on the beach by Tel Aviv when my stressful thinking finally conked out (see the previous chapter "total-orgasmicbliss" for more).

This is what sometimes happens when we're with our beloved and have a really good orgasm. Just think about it. In those few glorious moments before, during and after, what is your experience? Total bliss, right? Your mind is blank, right? And you experience a few glorious moments of no thought, which is a welcome respite from all your worries about the past or the future. Suddenly, it's all gone and you are simply and totally present in the moment. There's nothing else. Only this, only now, now, now. There's nothing you want, nothing to achieve, nothing to do. You are in bliss. Bliss! This bliss, which comes forth when your thinking momentarily stops, is in fact your true nature. And it feels great. Truly great! Yes, we call it love and the joy of being!

No wonder we want more of it.

No wonder we want to stay in this blissful state.

No wonder we attach having this experience to being with this particular person because this is where we experienced it. The state did arise when we were with this person. But the reality is, it's not the person who brought it to you, it's the lack of your own thinking that allows you to experience your true nature; which is this love, this joy, this bliss.

Of course, there are other situations in our lives where we experience peak moments like this—moments when our thinking stops and we are fully present and blissful.

Athletes experience it when they are fully present, focusing on their game. Runners experience it and call it "runners high". In fact, any activity where you enter "the zone" gives you a glimpse of this blissful state because your thinking conks out. The stressful thoughts and stories leave you alone for a while, and then, there you are, just like the sun, shining forth. It feels extremely blissful.

Peak moments can also arise when we're standing awestruck in nature, gazing at the beauty of a sunset or looking across the vast infinity of the ocean. Artists say they experience it at the height of their creativity, and we ordinary mortals taste it when we sing and dance with abandon or are completely absorbed in playing with a child.

Present in the now

All these experiences have one thing in common: they arise when we become so absorbed in whatever is happening that our stressful thinking momentarily stop, and then there's nothing but this. Then we are no longer attached to our thoughts and stories, but rather are fully aware of the present moment, of the now. Then we experience a glimpse of our true nature, which is love and joy.

But because most of us are not aware of this mechanism, we misunderstand the experience and believe the source of the love and bliss we are experiencing is the outer circumstance or the great sex or our partner. Obviously, since it's such a blissful experience, we naturally want more of it.

This is the basic misunderstanding: the misunderstanding that the source of the love and bliss we sometimes experience when we're with a partner is this person. This is the origin of "the mother of all relationship myths"—the myth that the love or happiness that we seek is outside us and dependent on another person.

The myth of romantic love

Another thing that really contributes to the strength and endurance of this myth is the fact that we all have been relentlessly programmed to believe in this idea since childhood. This idea—this myth—pervades our whole society. It's everywhere. We are constantly bombarded from all sides with the story that only a partner can make us truly happy. It's everywhere—in our pop songs, in our music videos, in the movies, on TV, in our books, art, and advertising, not to mention in the fashion and beauty industry. We've built a whole culture and lifestyle around this romantic idea. There are countless people working day and night in a wide variety of industries who are dedicated to helping make us attractive enough so that one day maybe we might be able to attract that one special person. That one special person who we believe is the key to experiencing the love and bliss we long for, for the rest of our lives. With such a massive onslaught of programming from all sides, it's no wonder that so many of us have bought into the myth without ever questioning it.

Yes, "the Devil" (our innocent confused thinking) has really done one hell of a job here!

But fortunately for us, there is help to be found. Once you finally become aware of this fundamental misunderstanding and how it arose, it becomes easier to see what's going on and experience the love and joy you seek, whether or not you have a partner by your side.

Meditation: Where does the love come from?

Here's a good exercise that can help you become more aware of where the love and joy you experience with your partner, really comes from:

Think of a time in your life where you experienced intense love. A time when you really felt love, bliss, a sense of safety, presence, oneness or whatever words you use to describe the experience of love. If you have not experienced this with a partner, then see if you can find some other situation where you experienced this feeling. It could be when you are with your child or with a really good friend or with your dog, or when you're out in nature or doing something that triggers this feeling in you.

Close your eyes and remember the experience in as many details as you can. Who was there, what it looked like, what you were doing and so on.

When you've done this, notice how this experience feels inside you, in your body. Maybe you feel warm, soft, relaxed, peaceful, safe…Open yourself to these feelings and bathe in them for a while.

Once you've bathed in these feelings for a little while, ask yourself where these feelings come from? Where does the feeling of love come from that you are experiencing right now? Who is having these feelings right now and who had those feelings when you first experienced them? You, right. Can there be a feeling and experience of love without you? Is it at all possible? Who, in fact, do these feelings belong to? You, right? And what triggered them right now as you sit here and read these words? Again, you! Yes, you. It's all about you.

It's all coming from you. Because where else could these feelings come from? As far as you are concerned, how can there be any experience of love or of anything else without you?

If you'd like to go deeper, try writing down how you would describe the experience of love. For example:

Totally present in the now
Timeless awareness
Open heart
Totally OK
Safe
Peaceful

Then for each word or feeling you wrote down, try to find at least three concrete examples of how you previously have experienced this feeling in your life —or how you are experiencing it in your life right now. It can be something big or little. For example, if you wrote "totally present in the now", your three situations might be: 1) Playing with my little nephew. 2) Walking on the beach at sunset. 3) Dancing.

Each time you find an example of how you already have this quality in your life, try to really feel what it feels like. What does it feel like to play intensely with your nephew? What does it feel like when you're walking on the beach at sunset? What does it feel like when you are really lost in dancing? Bathe for a while in these feelings.

The reason why this exercise is so powerful is that it can help you notice that the love that you seek is already in you. That it's already right here, right now in your life. The more you notice it and focus on it, the more you will experience it. Until one day you may notice that there is nothing but love in your life! The wind, the trees, the sun, the ocean, the earth you walk on, the bus you take to work, the bench you sit on in the park, all the people in your life, the air you breathe, the beating of your heart—is all love—in you and around you.

And yes, this is the great love.

RELATIONSHIP MYTHS

The love that I seek is outside me.

The love that I seek is dependent on another person.

The love and joy I experience when I am with my partner comes from my partner.

The love and joy I experience when I am with my partner is dependent on my partner.

Have you found
"the one and only"?

Recently one of my friends asked me if I wasn't dreaming of finding "the one and only" one for me—someone who really understands me, someone I really feel connected to, someone I can share my life and my dreams with.

I answered that I've already found "the one and only" one for me!

First of all, I said I've discovered that "the one and only" one for me *is* me, myself. I'm the one I'm with 24 hours a day, every day, seven days a week. I'm the one I go to bed with every evening and wake up with every morning. I'm the one who understands me better than anyone else in the whole world. I'm the one I feel more connected to than anyone else. I'm the one I always share my life and my dreams with—whether I notice it or not.

Second of all, I continued, I've also discovered that "the one and only" for me is the person I am with at any given moment. For example, I said to my friend, right now you're "the one and only" in my life. There is only you right now with me and here we are sitting in this beautiful café by the lake enjoying the swans and blue sky. That's all there is. Five minutes ago, when I stood at the counter and gave our order to the waitress and our eyes met briefly, she was "the one and only" in my life at that moment. Yesterday, when I was playing with my two-year-old nephew on the playground and I looked in his eyes, he was "the one and only" in my life. There was just him and me in that wonderful, magical moment of no time. A few days ago, when I was running on the beach with my brother's dog Tolle, well Tolle was "the one and only" one in my life at that moment. There were just the two of us, playing, out of breath and happy for no reason whatsoever. A year ago, when I was walking on the beach hand-in-hand with my beautiful ex-girlfriend watching the sun go down, she was "the one and only" one in my life then. And the person I'm going to give my attention to in the next moment will also be "the one and only" one in my life.

What about you? Have you found "the one and only" one for you?

Or are you still looking?

RELATIONSHIP MYTHS
"The one and only" one for me is outside myself.
I can only experience the love that I seek with one special person.

119

Why is it mainly women who are interested in self-help?

If you've ever been to a lecture, workshop, seminar, festival or other event in the world of self-help, personal development or spirituality, you've probably noticed an interesting phenomenon: there are many more women than men, often lots more.

My long and strange career as Tim Ray confirms this. During the past 15 years, I've given countless lectures and workshops in places like Stockholm, Copenhagen, Reykjavik, Prague, London (and even Charlotte, North Carolina!). In all these places, the male-female ratio has on average been about 90 percent women, 10 percent men.

If you've ever sent a manuscript to a publisher of self-help books, you also know that most of the editors for this type of book are women. Moreover, if you ask these editors who their core readers are, they'll say women, by far!

So there can be little doubt that many more women are interested in self-help and in doing "inner work" than men!

But why?

How can it be that so many more women are interested than men? Are women simply more conscious than men? Or what?

Here are some of my observations about why there are more women in the world of self-help and personal development than men:

One reason is that many women in their late 30s experience some kind of a crisis. (See the chapter "Stay away from women in their 30s" on page 25 for some of the reasons why.) Nothing motivates people like crisis to begin to look within and work with their inner states. So that's probably why we see so many women in that age group attending these events and reading this type of book.

But is that the only reason? Don't men also experience crises in their lives? Don't men also feel bad?

Yes, of course they do.

If this is true, then why is it that when men feel bad, not many of them look within and begin to do inner work as so many women do? I believe one of the main reasons is that we live in a society where it is still taboo for a man to be interested in his inner states, despite all the progress we've made when it comes to "women's liberation" and "men's liberation". The reality is that it's not so acceptable (or usual) for men to talk about how they feel, and especially not when they're with other men, while it's the exact opposite for women. If you're a woman, you are expected to be interested in and talk about your inner life, about your thoughts and feelings.

A good example of this is an interesting experience I had a couple of years ago during football practice with my (all male) team. Suddenly one of the players (a really tough, masculine guy) turned pale, stopped playing, and clutched his chest. Then he hobbled off the field and down to the locker room while we all watched. None of the other guys ran after him; instead, they just started playing again. I thought this was rather strange so I ran after him to see what was going on. To my great surprise, I found this hunk of a man stretched out on the floor in the locker room, looking very frightened. When I asked him what was going on, he said he was having an anxiety attack—something he apparently experienced now and again. So I just sat with him for a while and talked to him a bit and tried to get him to breathe deeply and relax. When he was feeling better, I went back to the other guys and asked them if this had ever happened before. (I was new on the team so I didn't know.) They replied, "Oh yeah, Jack sometimes has heart palpitations". But none of them would really look me in the eye or seemed to want to talk about it. It was like they were embarrassed— not for themselves but for him! Because anxiety attacks (as the hunk himself had just told me) were something only little old ladies have!

So what were the thoughts and beliefs that made this big, masculine teammate of mine feel so embarrassed about how he felt? What made it so hard for the other men to talk about it? I'm quite sure our classical myths about how a "real man" should be played a big part in their behavior. Myths that say:

- A real man doesn't cry.
- A real man doesn't show his feelings.
- It is a sign of failure if a real man feels bad.
- A real man should be big and strong.
- A real man shouldn't be weak and vulnerable.
- A real man doesn't talk about his feelings with others
  (especially not with other men).
- It is a sign of weakness if a man admits he made a mistake or apologizes.
- It is a sign of weakness if a man doesn't have all the answers.

I think it is the belief in these "gender myths" that is the main reason why we don't see so many men who are interested in self-help and personal development. Because unfortunately, these myths still prevent many men from daring to look at their own feelings and becoming more conscious of their inner lives.

This said, it is also true that we have seen some real change in the last decades in terms of our view of what it means to be a "real man". So even though it may still be a long way off, the traditional "macho man" (aka the "emotionally retarded man") is a dying race—at least here in the West. Fortunately we are seeing more men, especially from the younger generations in their 20s and 30s, attending events in the world of self-help and personal development. More men are beginning to show a bit more interest in their inner lives as well. In fact, after that day in the locker room, my teammate and I actually began to talk more. And when he discovered how interested I am in these matters, it turned out that he was too. He was quite interested in learning more about how his thinking affected him and his life.

So I believe—and sincerely hope—that in the coming years, we will see more and more men becoming involved in self-help, personal development and consciousness work—until the great day we attend some powerful personal development event and look around and see more men than women! Imagine that!

Are men and women
really different?

For many of us the idea that men and women are inherently different and communicate differently is one of our most precious beliefs and something we can spend endless hours discussing. We are simply fascinated by the idea. You know... "Men are from Mars... Women are from Venus... Men want one thing... Women want anothe... Men communicate like this... Women communicate like that..." And so on and so forth. As you've probably noticed, it's almost impossible to talk to anyone about relationships without the conversation at some point turning to the many key differences between women and men.

But is it really true? Is it really true that men and women are as different as so many of us believe?

If you take a closer look at the basic observations about the nature of reality and the way the mind works (see the Introduction and Part Two of this book), you will discover that every one of the observations about the nature of mind are equally true for both women and men.

Take, for example, the fundamental observation that all people are basically seeking the same thing—namely a happy life with no suffering. This is equally true for men and women. Everyone, whether male or female, in every culture and at every age, wants to live a happy life. No man or woman wants to suffer or be unhappy. This basic impulse or drive is something that motivates all human beings regardless of their gender (race, religion, age, social standing, etc.).

If you look closely at the way the mind works, you will also discover that the nature of mind is exactly the same for both women and men. Regardless of your gender, the nature of mind is that thoughts constantly arise and disappear again. This impersonal mechanism is the same whether you're a man or a woman. In addition, when a human being—again regardless of gender—believes a thought, then he or she gets to experience the effect of this thought (for better or for worse). Again, this is an unbreakable, impersonal mechanism that is 100 percent the same for men and women. This also means that since the minds of both men and women operate in exactly the same way, when our thinking is out of harmony with reality, the result is suffering whether you're a man or a woman.

The opposite is also equally true for both men and women. You can experience more happiness, love and peace — whether you are a man or a woman — by bringing your thinking and the focus of your attention back into harmony with reality.

Thus we see that the fundamental nature of every human being is the same for everyone, regardless of gender. When it comes to the nature of reality and the way the mind works, there's no difference between men and women.

Here gender makes no difference whatsoever.

Here there is total equality between the sexes!

Then why does it often seem that women and men are different!

If this is true, you may be thinking — if the fundamental nature of women and men is the same — how come it often seems that men and women are so different? How can it be that men and women often think, talk and act so differently?"

In order to answer this question it is important to remind ourselves of the underlying relationship between our thinking and our life experience. This underlying relationship or mechanism is *that there is a cause-and-effect-relationship between a person's thinking and his or her experience. Thought is cause, experience is effect.* This means that whatever a person believes affects his or her life and behavior — whether or not the beliefs are true.

So why is this so important?

OK let's say, for example, that from the moment a person was born, he or she was told that the Earth is flat. Everyone said so — parents, teachers, religion, society, the media — Yes, everyone. So as a result, this person then believes what he or she has been told and been brought up to believe. In this case, that the Earth is flat. What is the effect of this programming? Well as history has shown, people programmed like this did believe that the Earth *is* flat because nothing ever contradicted the idea and no one questioned it. In turn, this belief affected the way these people lived their lives. In this case, people were afraid to sail too far away from the coastline because they believed they would fall off the edge of the Earth down into some great abysmal nothingness. This was something most people believed until 500 years ago when Christopher Columbus demonstrated that the Earth is actually round by sailing across the Atlantic Ocean to America. So yes, our beliefs greatly influence our behavior — whether or not they have anything to do with reality.

The same holds true when it comes to the belief that men and women are different. For thousands and thousands of years, we human beings have been programmed to believe in a collective myth that men and women are different. As a result, this myth has become an extremely powerful, self-fulfilling prophecy.

Just think about the ways in which, from the moment we are born, boys and girls in our society are programmed by their surroundings to believe that men and women are different. Even unborn baby girls are called "princesses" and "angels", while no one would ever dream of saying the same about boy babies! This programming continues in daycare centers where girls are encouraged to play "princess games", while the boys are encouraged to let loose in the pillow room. Toys are also designed based on gender stereotypes and the belief that little girls want to play house games while little boys want to play with action heroes and weapons or with "stuff that does something" like diggers and bulldozers. This massive gender programming continues unabated through our teenage years straight into adulthood where all this gets further fueled by a multitude of theories, therapists, books and courses à la John Gray's *Men Are from Mars, Women Are from Venus*.

New research demolishes the myth

The newest findings in gender research demolish the myth that men and women are inherently different. "The Gender Similarities Hypothesis" from 2005 is one of the most comprehensive and important studies in recent times about the gender differences between men and women. The study was conducted by Janet Shibley Hyde, a professor of Psychology and Women's Studies at the University of Wisconsin-Madison. Published first in *American Psychologist* in 2005, the study is based on 20 years of comprehensive studies of the psychological differences between men and women. Hyde and her colleagues' study is based on a whopping 46 "meta-analyses" of the differences between men and women. Hyde explains, "Meta-analysis is a statistical method for aggregating research findings across many studies of the same question. It is ideal for synthesizing research on gender differences, an area in which often dozens or even hundreds of studies of a particular question have been conducted." So meta-analysis was the procedure researchers used to review thousands of studies to determine whether a hypothesis is true or not. Thus the basis of Professor Hyde's study is *very* comprehensive indeed.

Professor Hyde writes about her study; "The gender similarities hypothesis stands in stark contrast to the differences model, which holds that men and women, and boys and girls, are vastly different psychologically. The gender similarities hypothesis states, instead, that males and females are alike on most—but not all—psychological variables. Extensive evidence from meta-analyses of research on gender differences supports the gender similarities hypothesis. A few notable exceptions are some motor behaviors (e.g. throwing distances) and some aspects of sexuality, which show large gender differences. Aggression shows a gender difference that is moderate in magnitude."

In the study, Hyde observed the differences between men and women in a wide range of areas such as cognitive variables, verbal/nonverbal communication, social/personality variables, psychological well-being, motor behaviors, and miscellaneous constructs and concluded that: "The striking result is that 30% of the effect sizes are in the close-to-zero range, and an additional 48% are in the small range. That is, 78% of gender differences are small or close to zero."

The study also showed that in the cases where there were differences between men and women, these differences were usually moderate. Only in a very few cases were the differences between men and women really noticeable As stated above, the greatest difference discovered was that men can throw faster and further than women. It is also interesting to note that most of the meta-analyses addressed areas in which gender differences were reputed to be reliable such as mathematics performance and found that the gender differences in these areas were close to zero or very small. This is quite in contrast to popular belief!

Social programming

Not only did the study show that differences between women and men in most cases is either non-existent or very small, in those cases where there are moderate differences, the study demonstrates that these differences could very well be the result of social programming.

For example, the study showed that girls generally perform better in math than boys in elementary school and junior high, but this changes in high school. What is the cause of this gradual change in the mathematical abilities of teenage girls and boys? As the study points out, because of our collective belief that boys are better at math than girls, many parents often encourage sons more when it comes to supporting their children's mathematical prowess. As the study also demonstrated, parents' expectations about their children's mathematical skills can have a great influence on their self-confidence and on how well they do in math. "Girls may find their confidence in their ability to succeed in challenging math courses or in a mathematically oriented career undermined by parents' and teachers' beliefs that girls are weak in math ability," says Hyde.

In other words, the study shows that the strengths and weaknesses of boys and girls and of men and women are not necessarily inherent in human nature but can very well be the result of the gender prejudices that children of both sexes are exposed to from a very early age. Because, as the study also points out, if there really is a difference between girls' and boys' abilities, then these differences should be "stable". In other words, they should not change during the course of a man or woman's lifetime. But the study showed: "Gender differences grow larger or smaller at different times in the life span, and meta-analysis is a powerful tool for detecting these trends. Moreover, the fluctuating magnitude of gender differences at different ages argues against the differences model and notions that gender differences are large and stable."

Gender differences can be manipulated

Another thing the study demonstrates is that simple manipulation can create, erase or even reverse gender differences. "In one experiment, male and female college students with equivalent math backgrounds were tested. In one condition, participants were told that the math test had shown gender difference in the past, and in the other condition, they were told that the test had been shown to be gender fair — that men and women had performed equally well on it. In the condition in which participants had been told that the math test was gender fair, there were no gender differences in performance on the test. In the condition in which participants expected gender differences, women underperformed compared with men. This simple manipulation of context was capable of creating or erasing gender differences in math performance."

This experiment is very significant because it shows how quickly our collective and personal prejudices about gender differences can become self-fulfilling prophecies that powerfully influence self-confidence and performance.

Similar experiments in areas such as aggression and heroic rescue (two areas where we collectively believe men are stronger) and helping that is nurturing and caring such as caring for children (areas where we collectively believe women are stronger) showed how powerful our prejudices and expectations of gender roles can in determining a person's behavior. In this connection, it is interesting to note that men are more likely to live up to the role of the heroic rescuer when they know they are being watched (when there are onlookers). From Hyde's study: "Meta-analysts have addressed the importance of context for gender differences… Heroic helping involves danger to the self, and both heroic and chivalrous helping are facilitated when onlookers are present."

Other experiments also showed that the differences between men and women varied greatly depending on whether they were being observed — and especially if they knew they were being observed. For example, when men knew they were being observed, they were more helpful than women. But when there were no onlookers, this difference disappeared! The same thing was discovered about smiling. When women knew they were being observed, they smiled more than they did when they were not aware of being observed! This is very interesting because it shows that it's not just our thoughts about what it means to be a man or a woman that affect our behavior, but also how we believe others expect us to act based on our sex!

"The conclusion is clear," says Hyde. "The magnitude and even the direction of gender differences depend on the context. These findings provide strong evidence against the differences model and its notions that psychological gender differences are large and stable."

Harmful to our health!

Not only does Hyde's study demonstrate that our collective myths about gender differences are not based on scientific fact, she also points out that the consequences of these myths are often very limiting and even harmful for both sexes.

One consequence of the highly exaggerated claims of differences between women and men is the stereotypical idea that women are better nurturers and caretakers than men. For men, this belief can inhibit a man's ability to be nurturer (both of himself and others) — and even affect his ability to take care of his own children.

At the workplace, this myth can also have far-reaching consequences. Because of our beliefs, women who are competent and powerful are also expected to live up to the female stereotype of being sweet, feminine and nurturing at the same time. If they are not, they may be viewed as non-emphatic and insensitive bosses because they don't live up to the stereotypical idea of nurturing women regardless of their professional competencies. This rarely happens to a man who is competent at his profession. Thus gender stereotypes may lead to powerful women being criticized for traits men would seldom be criticized for. "The persistence of the stereotype of women as nurturers leads to serious costs for women who violate this stereotype in the workplace," points out Hyde.

Harmful for our relationships too!

Relationships are another area where the study showed that the belief in differences between men and women can have very serious, negative consequences. One of our biggest collective relationship myths is the belief that men and women communicate in very different ways. John Gray's mega-bestseller *Men are from Mars,*

Women are from Venus, is based on this myth. Interestingly enough, since its release in 1992, the book has sold more than 30 million copies worldwide and is now translated into 40 languages. As the title of the book implies, Gray's message is based on the assumption that men and women communicate so differently it is as if they come from different planets.

Thus it is interesting to note that the Gender Similarities Hypothesis demonstrates that when it comes to communication, there is no difference between women and men! According to the study, there is no scientific evidence to support the claim that women and men have difficulty communicating with each other. Hyde says that not only is there no scientific evidence whatsoever to support the claims in Gray's book, she points out that relationships between men and women can suffer greatly when people believe that men and women talk different languages! "When relationship conflicts occur, good communication is essential to resolving the conflict," says Hyde. "If, however, women and men believe what they have been told — that it is almost impossible for them to communicate with each other — they may simply give up on trying to resolve the conflict through better communication. Therapists will need to dispel erroneous beliefs in massive, unbridgeable gender differences."

Hyde concludes her study as follows: "The scientific evidence does not support the belief that men and women have inherent difficulties in communicating across genders…. Therapists who base their practice in the differences model should reconsider their approach on the basis of the best scientific evidence."

Professor Hyde is far from alone in her observations that the erroneous presentation of gender differences in our society is without basis in reality and can have harmful consequences for men and women of all ages. In 2005 the American Psychological Association (APA) sent out a press release in support of the study and quotes Hyde as follows: "The claims can hurt women's opportunities in the workplace, dissuade couples from trying to resolve conflict and communication problems and cause unnecessary obstacles that hurt children and adolescents' self-esteem."

So why is the myth still alive and kicking?

If there is no scientific evidence to support the belief in gender differences, why are these facts not more commonly known in our society today? Why is the myth of gender differences, despite all our so-called "progress" in gender equality, still alive and kicking?

In an article in *Psychology Today*, the American social psychologist and author Daisy Grewall writes that the truth about the sexes just doesn't sell as well as the myth of gender differences. According to Grewall, this is why the media, the advertising industry, and even the "self-help" industry often turn a blind eye to the truth. Apparently the myth of gender differences is more "sexy" than the truth that men and women are the same! But just how sexy is it when women's opportunities are limited in the workplace? How sexy is it when a man's ability to nurture his own children is questioned? Or when the mathematical skills of girls are overlooked and played down? Or when relationships between men and women become more problematic than necessary because people believe they can't communicate with each other?

This doesn't sound very sexy to me!

So let's get real about who we really are! If you're in doubt about the truth of the matter, I highly recommend taking a closer look at the Gender Similarities Hypothesis. Not only is it fascinating reading but it clearly shows that the claims of gender differences are widely overrated, even in areas where most people traditionally think of men and women as different. The study also demonstrates that in the areas where there are some differences between the sexes, it is usually not an inherent difference but rather a difference that has arisen from generations of social programming. So hopefully Hyde's excellent work will be the beginning of the end of one of the biggest of all myths when it comes to men, women and relationships.

Just think about it! Who would you be if you no longer believed in the myth that men and women are different? Wouldn't it radically change your view of yourself, your partner and relationships?

RELATIONSHIP MYTHS
Men and women are different.
Men and women communicate differently.
Men and women don't understand each other.
Men and women can't understand each other.
Men and women have difficulty talking to each other.
Men are better than women at _____.
Women are better than men at _____.
Men are _____.
Women are _____.

Interlude

Interlude:
The Devil is worried
...really worried

It was a completely ordinary, burning hot afternoon in Hell when the Devil received a very unusual bit of news. Actually, it was the most surprising and worrying bit of news His Most Diabolical Highness had received in several thousand years.

When the news arrived, the Devil was busy tormenting the latest sending of men and women who had landed in Hell because they innocently believed in the Devil's lies about love and relationships. This was a regular occurrence in Hell because after the Devil's Sales and Marketing people had launched his super-duper-mega-giga advertising campaign about "the one and only" and "soul mates", things were really going well with the Devil's mission, which was *to make as many people as possible, as unhappy as possible, for as long as possible."* In fact, his mission had succeeded beyond even his wildest dreams and for thousands of years now, most of humanity had been feeling confused, unhappy and lonely because of the Devil's many lies about love and relationships. Things were going so well with the Devil & Co.'s ingenious plan that his global corporation had long been listed on the New York Stock Exchange. Now he was even cooking up plans to conquer other planets in the galaxy!

But then, just as the Devil was about to assemble his diabolical Storm Troopers from Hell to launch his ambitious galactic plans for expansion, the unsettling news arrived!

It was none other than Frank Sinatra, the Devil's most successful ambassador when it came to promoting lies about love and relationships, who reluctantly agreed to deliver the news to the Devil. Yes, Good Ol' Blue Eyes knew it would be a difficult task, so before he actually went, he tried to muster up his courage by singing "Let's Face the Music & Dance" over and over again, but it didn't help much. Now, as the great crooner stood before his Devilish Master in all his Diabolical Horror, he felt more than just a little nervous. Frankie Boy was well aware that the Devil might just be a trifle upset by the news, to put it mildly.

"Sorry to disturb you, Your Most Diabolical Highness, in the middle of your afternoon torture session, but some rather … how shall I say … unsettling news has just come in from the surface of the Earth," said Frankie Boy with a trembling voice.

"Unsettling?" said the Devil, without looking up from the piles of men and women he was enjoying torturing with one of his favorite lies that *the love that you seek is dependent on another person.* "Unsettling? Well what do you mean by unsettling?"

"Well, umm…" mumbled Frankie Boy nervously. "I mean…"

"You mean what? For Heaven's sake—out with it, my boy!"

"God has sent an Archangel to Earth," said Frankie Boy starring at the glowing hot stone floor.

"An Archangel?" For the first time, the Devil looked up from his afternoon torture session. This was a bit of news. "Which Archangel? Gabriel? Michael?"

"No, no," said Frankie Boy shaking his head, still looking down.

"Well then, who? The Archangel of Love? The Archangel of Enlightenment?"

"No, not them either."

"Damn it to Heaven, Frankie Boy! Tell me who for Hell's sake!"

"It's the Archangel…" small beads of sweat were visible on his forehead," It's the Archangel of Sanity!"

"What!!!" The Devil sprang up so quickly from his red-hot throne that giant balls of fire shot out in all directions from his fifteen arms. "The Archangel of Sanity! It can't be true!"

"Yes, Your Most Diabolical Highness, I assure you, it's true…" stuttered Frankie Boy as he slowly started backing out of the throne room. "The information comes from our most reliable sources…"

"The Archangel of Sanity! It simply can't be true…" cried the Devil, shaking all his heads. The Archangel of Sanity hadn't been seen on Earth for many thousands of years now—which was why things had been going so well for the Devil's many lies about love and relationships.

"Sanity, Sanity!" roared the Devil and sat down on his flaming throne and took a deep breath. The last time the Archangel of Sanity had been on Earth, everything went wrong with the Devil's mission plan *to make as many people as possible, as unhappy as possible, for as long as possible.* As soon as the Archangel of Sanity appeared on Earth, people everywhere started to regain their sanity and began questioning the Devil's many lies. It was a catastrophe! In a very short time, Sanity spread like wildfire in the collective consciousness of humanity and the Devil & Co. came upon hard times indeed, very hard times.

Now the Archangel of Sanity was back! After several thousand years of absence from Earth!

The Devil slowly turned his most fiendish glare in the direction of the old crooner and said very, very slowly, "What more can you tell me?"

By now, Ol' Blue Eyes had nearly backed himself all the way out of the Devil's fortified and fiery throne room, but the Devil was quicker than Frankie Boy, yanking him back before his fiery throne. "Tell me!" roared the Devil so loudly that all the doors to Hell shook, "tell me what He's up to now!"

"Well, er... "stammered Frankie Boy, looking very pale, "it seems the Archangel is spreading Sanity very quickly when it comes to love and relationships..."

"WHAT!!" roared the Devil even louder than before, "I don't believe it!" For thousands of years now, the Devil's many lies about love and relationships had been the main weapons the Devil used to lure men and women into Hell. It had simply been His Master Plan — the plan of plans, which had succeeded so phenomenally that the Devil & Co. was on the verge of galactic expansion. And then what happens...

"I am sorry to say so, Your Most Diabolical Highness, but it's true..." said Frankie Boy softly. "More and more people on Earth are returning to their Sanity."

"Already?" snorted the Devil. "How in Heaven could this have happened?"

Frankie Boy looked around to make sure no one else could hear what he was going to say. Then he whispered, "It seems that the Archangel of Sanity has written some kind of manual — you know a guidebook or something — on what you can do about the many lies Your Most Diabolical Highness has been promoting."

"A manual?"

"Yes, Your Most Diabolical Highness," said Frankie Boy, looking around again, "and one of my very own Hellish envoys has managed to get a copy of it."

"A copy?"

"Yes, Your Most Diabolical Highness," said Frankie Boy proudly.

"Well then let me see it for Hell's Sake," roared the Devil.

Frankie Boy took the little book out of his inside pocket and put it in the Devil's huge fiery paw.

Then the Devil leaned back on his red hot throne and looked quietly at the little book for a very long moment — and then slowly, very slowly he opened the book and began to read the first page...

How to Stop Them from Sabotaging Your Happiness

MYTHBUSTING *[mith-bust-ing]: to investigate a myth (thought, belief, story) to find out whether it is in harmony with reality or not.*

Mythbusting 101

If you recognize yourself in some of the chapters in Part One of this book and see that you sometimes believe in and are run by some of our collective myths about relationships that sabotage our happiness — well don't despair! The good news is you can do something about it. It's really quite simple (although it may not always be easy in practice!).

Because the truth is relationship myths happen to be just that — myths! They are legends, tall tales and gossip, which are passed down from generation to generation. They have nothing to do with reality. The more you can see and understand that these relationship myths really have nothing to do with reality, the more you can begin to live in harmony with the way things are. When this happens, you will experience more of the joy and love that you seek.

That's exactly what this part of the book is about — how to do it. You can do it with the simple, practical tools I describe here. Tools you can use here and now to investigate and "mythbust" the thoughts and beliefs about relationships that are making you unhappy.

So let's get started! There's no time to waste when it comes to love and your happiness!

The first step in effective mythbusting is:

Identify the thought

Before you can investigate if a relationship belief has anything to do with reality, you must be able to identify the belief or story that upsets you. So, you must catch it first and write it down. If you don't write it down, you'll probably forget the thought immediately and be carried away by the next thought that pops up.

Sometimes it's not difficult to find out what the thought or belief is that stresses you. You may feel ill at ease or unhappy, but not quite sure what the thought or thoughts are that are causing the feeling of discomfort.

But even though it may be difficult for you to pinpoint the thought or thoughts that lie behind your discomfort, that doesn't mean that there's no thought behind it. There's *always* a thought behind every feeling of discomfort. Remember the second basic observation that I outlined in the Introduction:

There is a cause-and-effect-relationship between your thinking and your experience. Thought is cause, experience is effect.

This means that you can't have an emotion without believing a thought first. This is very important, so I am going to repeat this: *You cannot have an emotion without believing a thought first.* You cannot feel anger without first believing a thought that makes you angry. You cannot feel sad without first believing a thought that makes you sad. You cannot feel anxiety or discomfort without first believing thoughts that make you anxious and uncomfortable. Because thought is cause and your emotions, your actions and your experience are the effect.

Despite the fact that thought is cause and emotion is effect, the first thing we usually notice is the emotion. But this doesn't mean there's no thought behind it. There always is. It's just that we're not always aware of what that thought is. There are several reasons for this.

One reason is that many of us are just not particularly aware of what we are thinking at any time. This is because we all think hundreds of thoughts an hour, but how many of these thoughts are we actually aware of? Usually not that many.

Another reason is that when we feel discomfort in some situation like in our relationship, it's often not just because of one thought, but because of several or many thoughts and beliefs which we are usually unconscious of. It may not just be thoughts about the present situation; it can be other thoughts as well… thoughts about love in general and about relationships and human interactions. This also explains why we sometimes go ballistic about something quite insignificant — because it triggers so many thoughts…

So yes, it's important to see that there's always a thought or several thoughts behind every feeling of discomfort. To be an effective mythbuster, the first step is to learn to identify the thought or thoughts behind the discomfort that you are experiencing in your relationship.

Pain is a warning signal

One could say that every feeling of discomfort is an alarm signal from within which lets you know you are believing a thought or story that is in opposition to reality. The further away from reality the thought is, and the more you believe it, the more it hurts. But the hurt is actually a good thing. It's like putting your hand in the fire. The pain you feel is actually a good thing, because if it didn't hurt, your whole hand might get burned off! So the pain is actually your friend. It's a warning signal.

It's the same when you feel discomfort, anxiety, anger or sadness. You can be sure it's a sign that your thinking is out of harmony with reality. And it's time to investigate your thoughts.

How to identify the thought behind the emotion

If you're feeling discomfort or are unhappy in your relationship but are having difficulty pinpointing the thought or thoughts that lie behind the feeling, you can do the following:

Close your eyes and be still and then focus your attention on the feeling of discomfort. Instead of trying to get the feeling to go away, welcome it and enter it. Imagine that the feeling of discomfort is like a small frightened, confused child, and that you're the child's mother or father. If your child was unhappy and crying, you wouldn't just kick it out onto the street, would you? No, you'd probably take it into your arms, hug it and try to understand it. You would talk to your child. So do the same thing with the feeling of discomfort you're experiencing. Have a little talk with it and ask the feeling why it's so upset. Then write down the answers that come to you. Perhaps the feeling will say: "If he really loves me, he'll do what I want" or "She doesn't love me because..." or "He shouldn't spend so much time in front of the computer". Perhaps you'll become aware of one or many thoughts. Write them all down. Don't censor yourself no matter how stupid or absurd the thoughts may seem.

If you've written down many thoughts, you can circle the ones that are the most painful and begin by investigating them. If you're up for it, you can investigate the remaining thoughts later.

Another good way to identify the thoughts about relationships that stress you is to notice if you feel discomfort when reading one of the chapters in Part One. If you do, it may be a sign that you're suffering from the relationship myth or myths the chapter describes. To make it easier for you, I've listed the thoughts and myths that are usually behind our feelings of discomfort at the end of most chapters. So you can work on them.

Now that you have identified the thoughts and myths you want to investigate you're ready for mythbusting!

Mythbusting — the short version

So, based on everything you've learned in this book, here is my basic mythbusting formula, condensed into five easy steps you can use anytime, anywhere.

MYTHBUSTING
Five steps to feeling better in your relationship immediately!

1) Understand that your thinking is the reason why you feel like you do.
2) Notice what you are thinking when you feel upset.
3) Notice the difference between the thought and reality.
4) Notice how you feel when you stick to reality.
5) Make regular reality checks.

Sounds good right! OK, so let's look a little more closely at the five steps.

1) Understand that your thinking is the reason why you feel like you do.
Remind yourself that it's your thinking and your interpretations of what your partner says and does that are making you unhappy — and nothing else.

2) Notice what you are thinking when you feel upset.
When you are upset, write the thought or thoughts down that are bothering you. Let's take an example. OK, so it's a nice, sunny Saturday and you want to go for a hike in the woods today with your girlfriend. When you ask her, she says no, she doesn't want to go because she wants to meet her girlfriends at a café for brunch. You are surprised at how upset you feel when she says no and when you look for the thought or thoughts behind the feeling, you discover the belief: "If she really loves me, she'll do what I want."

3) Notice the difference between the thought and reality.
OK, so now that you've identified the thought that's upsetting you, let's look at it and compare it to reality. What is the reality in relation to this thought? The reality is your girlfriend doesn't want to go hiking in the woods with you today — but does that really mean she doesn't love you? No, probably not. (She didn't say she wanted a divorce or was moving out, did she?) And if she really does love you, does that mean she "should" go hiking with you in the woods today? What does hiking in the woods have to do with her loving you? When you look at reality, you'll discover that the reality is people who love each other often have different desires and preferences.

Noticing this means that you are getting real about what's going on. Noticing this means that you are looking clearly at the reality of what's going on without making assumptions about what things may or may not mean and without linking things together that have nothing to do with each other. When you look at reality, you can see that an afternoon hike in the woods is one thing; loving each other is another. Or you could put it like this: Having different preferences is one thing; loving each other is another thing. Looking carefully at this is a good way to stay real.

4) Notice how you feel when you stick to reality.

Who would you be if you acknowledged reality and lived in harmony with it in relation to your partner? If you can now see the fact that yes, the reality is that your partner does sometimes have different preferences than you do but this has nothing to do with her love for you, how does that makes you feel? Hmmm. Much more relaxed right? Hmmm. Much more lighthearted, right? Much more able to see and feel that well, yes, she'd rather go to a café for brunch with her girlfriends than go hiking with me today but, what the heck, it's not the end of the world. She still loves me. Life is good. I guess I'll call my friend Mike and ask him if he wants to go with me.

5) Make regular reality checks.

Make regular reality checks during the course of your day and investigate the thought or thoughts that are upsetting you with this simple mythbusting technique. Notice what happens to you when your thoughts or stories don't match the reality that's right in front of your eyes. Then get real and bring yourself back to reality.

Expectations & reality

Another really good way to become more aware of the difference between reality and your thinking when it comes to your relationship is this technique by Barbara Berger called *Expectations & Reality*. (For more about this technique see our book "The Awakening Human Being—A Guide to the Power of Mind" by Barbara Berger with Tim Ray).

Here's what to do. Get out a paper and pen and write down the name of your partner. If you're not in a relationship at the moment, write down the name of your ex-partner. (If you're one of the few people on the planet who's never been in a relationship, write down the name of your mother or father—in the final analysis it doesn't make much difference!)

The exercise has four parts.

1) Expectations and wishes

Close your eyes and think of three things you think your partner should do (or not do) to make your relationship better. Three things which you are unsatisfied with. Three things you would like to have your partner change. Three things you believe will make your relationship better. (If you are doing the exercise on your ex-partner, think of three things you thought at the time he or she should have done differently which would have made your relationship better.) Please be ruthlessly honest. You don't have to show your list to anyone.

Now open your eyes and write down the three things. Here are some examples of what you could write down:

He should be more interested in self-help and personal development.

He should play more with the children.

He should spend more time with me.

2) Reality

Now that you've written down the three things you think your partner should do (or should have done) to improve your relationship, close your eyes and take a look at the reality. What is the reality in relationship to what you wrote down? Honestly. What is the reality when it comes to your partner? Not what you think it should be. Not what you hope it will be. Not what you hope it will be one day if you work hard enough to change your partner or yourself. But what is the reality right here, right now in your relationship?

Is he interested in self-help and personal development? Does he read self-help books and go to lectures or courses? Is he working with himself? Do you talk about things like this together? When you look carefully, what do you see? Is the reality simply that your partner isn't interested in personal development, despite what you say? Remember — actions speak louder than words.

What about when it comes to playing with the kids. Does he play with them? Sometimes? Does he play with them as much as you think he should? Perhaps you will discover that he doesn't, regardless of how many times you've asked him to. The reality is he just doesn't play with the children as much as you want him to.

What about spending time with you? Does he spend as much time with you as you think he should? What is the reality? Again — not what you are hoping for or dreaming of, but what is actually going on right now. Be very thorough and scientific like you were a professor conducting an experiment or a judge in a courtroom. Maybe you will discover that yes, he does spend some time with you but not as much as you'd like no matter how much you ask him to. The reality is he's often busy with other things.

Now that you have discovered what the reality is in these three areas, write down what you discovered. Just the plain facts. For example:

He is not interested in self-help and personal development.

He doesn't play very often with the children.

He doesn't spend very much time with me.

3) Emotions

When you begin to see the difference between reality and your expectations a little more clearly in these three areas, the next step is to notice what feelings arise in you when you actually begin to see reality for what it is. So close your eyes and see how you feel when you look at the reality of who your partner is in the three areas you are investigating (or who your partner was if you are looking at a past relationship).

What feelings does it awaken in you when you see that the reality is that your partner just isn't interested in self-help and personal development? Do you feel peaceful and a sense of relief when you look reality in the eye, because you know it's hopeless to try to change him? Do you relax and feel OK about it? Or do you feel a real sense of sadness because you know in your heart that you really don't want to be with a person who is not interested in something which is so important for you?

What do you feel when you admit that your partner just doesn't play that much with your children? Do you feel peaceful about this? Can you accept this reality? Or are you angry and disappointed? Or do you feel all of these things at the same time? There are many possibilities.

What do you feel about the reality that your partner just doesn't spend as much time with you as you desire? Is this OK with you? Are you relaxed and at peace with the way things are? Or do you feel hurt and sad? Or angry? Or indifferent?

When you have discovered what you feel when you look at the way things really are, write your feeling down.

4) Action

The last step in this exercise is to explore what you will do and how you will act now, when you see the reality of your partner for what it is. (Or would have done in the past if you had seen the reality of your partner for what it was.) In other words, instead of basing your actions on unrealistic expectations as to how your partner should be, investigate how you will act and what you will do if you look realistically at this person and accept him or her for what he/she is.

What will you do if you see your partner for who he or she really is? How will you act? How will you treat your partner? How will you treat yourself? What will you do differently? Will you change your behavior? Or will the change be that you'll stop trying to change your partner and just let him or her alone? Close your eyes and consider the situation—and be open for new impulses.

So now that you see the reality that your partner just isn't interested in self-help and personal development, what will you do about it? Will you just leave him alone and concentrate on doing what you think is important and exciting? Will you stop giving him books to read and stop dragging him to lectures and courses? Will you go to that weekend course you've been dreaming about without him? Will you try to find other people who share your interests? Will you end the relationship because you don't want to be with someone who isn't interested in something that is so important for you?

What will you do when you recognize the reality that your partner doesn't play with children as much as you think he/she should. Will you have a serious talk with him and ask him to play more with kids? Or will you accept that that's just the way it is and then concentrate on playing with the children yourself?

What about the fact that your partner doesn't spend as much time with you as you would like? Will you stop pressing him to do so and focus instead on giving yourself the things you wanted your partner to give you? Will you give yourself the love and attention you want? Or will you you try to find other people who are interested in spending time with you and giving you what you want?

Again there are many possibilities. Be open and write down all the ideas that come to you. Don't censor yourself—this is just a list of possibilities and you don't have to show it or share it with anyone.

You can do this exercise again and again

This exercise or technique of comparing reality with your expectations is something you can do over and over again, just like my mythbusting technique. When you feel frustrated or unhappy with your partner or your relationship, write down your expectations and compare them to reality. Then explore how you would feel and act if your thinking about the situation was in harmony with reality.

You can also do this exercise with another person

It's also very enlightening to do this exercise with another person—for example with a close friend. (It's probably best not to do this with your partner unless you both are used to working with yourselves and are able to communicate honestly and openly with each other in this way.) When you do the exercise with a friend, you both write down your expectations when it comes to your partner (or ex-partner) and then take turns reading your answers aloud to each other. When working with another person like this, it is important to just listen to the other person without commenting or criticizing or judging what they say. Just let your friend explore and find his or her own truth. Once you have told each other about your expectations about your partners, then go on to the next step and write down what the reality is when it comes to your partners. Then again take turns sharing with each other what you have discovered. Do the same with steps 3 and 4.

Doing this exercise with another person can be a very powerful experience. Both because it can be very healing to tell another person how you really feel—and also because you can learn so much from hearing another person's expectations and reality.

Getting Real

You can also use this technique to investigate your expectations in relation to reality when it comes to your children, your parents, your friends and your colleagues. Once you have learned the technique, there are no limits to how you can use it. So give it a try and see what happens when you bring your thinking into harmony with reality!

This is what "Getting Real" is all about! (For more good "Getting Real" tools, see our book, *The Awakening Human Being, A Guide to the Power of Mind*).

The Work of Byron Katie

If you want to go even deeper in your investigation of the difference between reality and your thinking, I suggest you try the four questions of The Work of Byron Katie. The Work is very simple yet amazingly effective, not least when it comes to relationship problems.

First you identify the thought, belief or story that is making you unhappy and write it down on a piece of paper. Then you investigate the thought with the following four questions:

1. Is it true?
2. Can you absolutely know that it's true?
3. How do you react when you believe that thought?
4. Who would you be without the thought?
   Turn the thought around.

Let's take an example and investigate it using the four questions of The Work. Let's say you feel unhappy because of the thought: *My partner should understand me!* So first you write the thought down and then you investigate it. So let's try it.

1. Is it true?

Again, the first and most important step is obviously to investigate if a thought has anything to do with reality. In other words, is this thought true or not? This makes a pretty big difference — like is the earth flat or round?

So with this question, you are asking yourself — perhaps for the first time in your life — if a thought or belief is actually true. You're asking if this thought has anything whatsoever to do with reality.

Take your time when you ask yourself this question and see what comes up from deep inside you. You are looking for your answer. Not what you've learned from other people. Not what you may have believed your whole life. But what your genuine answer is right now.

Is it true that *your partner should understand you?*

If your answer is yes, then go on to question 2. If your answer is no, go on to question 3.

2. Can you absolutely know that it's true?

If you answered yes to question 1, try to go deeper and ask yourself if you absolutely can know with 100 percent certainty that this thought is true.

When you do this, really give yourself time to feel your truth. You may discover that you can't absolutely know with 100 percent certainty that *your partner should understand you*. Because when you look closely, what in fact is the reality? Does your partner always understand you? No! He or she doesn't! That's the reality. Do you always understand yourself? Probably not either! So if you don't even understand yourself that well, how can you expect your partner to understand you? Is your partner inside your head? Can your partner experience your thoughts, your feelings or your body? No, of course not! So the answer to this question is probably no, you can't absolutely know your partner should understand you since the reality is he or she often doesn't!

3. How do you react when you believe that thought?

Once you've investigated whether the thought is true or not, the next step is to notice the cause-and-effect relationship between your belief in a thought and your experience. In other words, now it's time to become more aware of how believing a thought affects you. When you believe a thought, it always has an effect on you.

Believing a thought is something like what happens if you put your hand in the fire — you feel something, don't you? Well it's the same when you believe thoughts that don't correspond to reality — they hurt. And this affects your feelings, your body, your behavior, the way you treat yourself and other people.

So how does it affect you when you believe the thought that *your partner should understand you* and he or she doesn't always understand you?

When you ask yourself this question you might discover that you feel angry and hurt. Or you might think your partner is selfish and only thinks about him or herself. Maybe you even begin to question whether or not your partner really does love you (if this happens, write down this thought and investigate it later). Or maybe when you believe this thought, you become cold and withdrawn and close your heart to your partner. Maybe you snap at your partner and yes... all these things feel uncomfortable.

Another good way to observe what the belief in this thought does to you is to ask yourself whose business are you minding when you believe this thought? Whose business is it what your partner thinks and feels? Is it your business or your partner's? Whose business is it what your partner does and doesn't do, understands and doesn't understand? It's your partner's business! Obviously! Whose business is it what you think, feel, do and don't do? Well, that's your business. So notice what happens when you are in your partner's business and try to control what your partner understands and doesn't understand. Notice that you are trying to do the impossible! Yes, it's impossible to control what your partners thinks, feels and understands. That's why it hurts so much when you try—it's hopeless!

You may also notice that when you are minding your partner's business, there's no one at home to take care of you! No one to understand you! This is something which can really make you feel lonely and abandoned. This, in turn, can release a chain of dysfunctional behaviors like binge eating or drinking or smoking.

So allow yourself time to explore the many ways believing this thought affects you and your life.

4. Who would you be without the thought?

The next step is to explore how you would feel and how your life would be if you no longer believed the thought. For many people this can be quite a new experience because they are so used to completely believing their thoughts. But if you are willing to try this and dare really listen and explore what you feel, you may be surprised at the insights that arise.

So when you ask yourself who you would be without the thought that *your partner should understand you*, the answer could be that you will see your partner in a completely new light. Without this thought, you might feel more love and affection for your partner because you would no longer equate love with understanding one and other. Or you might find that without the thought you are able to set your partner free to be whoever he or she is. So you might feel a sense of relief... which feels quite peaceful and loving.

Maybe you will discover that your relationship becomes more exciting because it becomes more of a mystery, more of an adventure and you start looking to see if you can "connect" beyond words. There are many possibilities. So just sit with the question and allow whatever comes to come. You might be pleasantly surprised!

Turn the thought around

After you have investigated the thought that is bothering you with the four questions, it is time to turn the thought around to its direct opposite. Then investigate whether the opposite of the original thought could be as true or truer than what you started with. There are several ways you can turn around the original thought *my partner should understand me.* Here are some examples:

My partner shouldn't understand me.
Could this be as true or truer? When you look at this thought, you will probably see that yes, it could be just as true or truer than the original thought. Because what's the reality? The reality is probably that sometimes your partner doesn't understand you. See if you can find at least three concrete examples of why this is true. For example:

1. My partner doesn't know how it feels to be me when I am at work.
2. My partner doesn't know how it feels to be me when I have a migraine headache.
3. My partner doesn't know how it felt to grow up in my family, with my parents.

Here's another way in which you can turn around the original thought:

I should understand my partner.
Could this be as true or truer? When you investigate this more closely you may find that there could be some truth in this too. Firstly, when you believe the thought that your partner should understand you — and the reality is he or she doesn't — well then you are NOT understanding your partner! Funny, isn't it? It turns out that you don't understand that your partner doesn't understand you! Maybe it's not so easy to follow the advice you are giving your partner (that *he/she should understand me)* as you thought. Maybe you can even find ways in which you can try harder to understand how your partner feels! For example:

1. I should understand that my partner doesn't understand me.
2. I should understand that it's not so easy for my partner to understand me as I thought.
3. If I want my partner to understand me, I should learn to better communicate how I feel, and what I want from my partner.
4. I could double my efforts to try understanding how my partner feels about his/her life, work situation, family, friends, feelings, etc.

Here's a third way you can turn around the original thought:

I should understand me!
Could this be as true or truer? If you become very quiet and notice how this feels, you will probably discover that this could be a lot truer than the original statement too. Because when you think about it, who has the best chance of understanding you? Of understanding how you think, feel and experience life? You do, of course! Because you're the person you are closer to than anyone else. You're the person you spend twenty-four hours a day with and wake up with every morning. So yes, it's your job to understand you. When you're so busy trying to get your partner to understand you, you forget to do your job—which is for you to *understand you!* So again, try to find three concrete examples of how you should understand you, such as:

1. I should understand me because I know how it feels to be me at work.
2. I should understand me because I know how it feels when I have a migraine—and I know what I need to do to feel better.
3. I should understand me because I know exactly how it felt to grow up in my family with my parents.

Four questions that can change your life

When you investigate a thought using these four questions, you will probably experience several things. Firstly, you will find that your belief or attachment to the thought becomes progressively less. Secondly, you will discover that the discomfort and pain you feel in connection with the thought also becomes progressively less. Thirdly, by investigating who you would be without the thought, you will discover new and more constructive and healthy sides of yourself, your life and your partner. All of which will change your life—and your experience of your relationship—for the better.

A gradual process

When you begin investigating your thinking in this way, it's important to realize that learning to see through and release yourself from stressful thoughts in this way is a gradual process. It doesn't happen overnight but is something you have to work on day after day, month after month. This of course is why this method is called "The Work"! It's not a miracle cure or miracle pill you can take once and then never need to investigate your thinking again.

What happens for most people is that when they investigate stressful thoughts, they begin to experience more clarity and a little less attachment to these thoughts. But this first breakthrough doesn't necessarily mean that these stressful thoughts will never come back again (they usually do) nor that we'll never believe in them again. What does happens is that the next time we notice these thoughts, we find we believe in them a little less — and that we're a little less attached to them, a little less identified with them. Because of that, we also feel better.

If you have investigated a thought and still feel that it is very painful the next time it arises, the best thing you can do is investigate it again. Ask the four questions again and try to go deeper. Try to be more open and allow whatever comes up to come up. I find that the four questions are like powerful deep sea divers you are sending deep into your inner world to find the wisdom that is hiding within you! Every time you do The Work, you go a little deeper and come up a little clearer!

If you continue to do this, you will discover that the next time the thought arises you believe in it a little less, until the day finally comes (maybe after you've investigated the thought many times) that you no longer experience any discomfort anymore. You simply see the thought for what it is — an old wives' tale, a myth that you once innocently believed — until the day finally comes that when the thought appears, you simply laugh at it.

It's like saying the earth is flat — yeah, right!

So… *My partner should understand me* — yeah, right!

For more about The Work, see Byron Katie's books, especially her first book *Loving What Is*, which offers a detailed explanation of how to do The Work in all areas of one's life.

Being together in the silence

Most of us have probably at some time or other tried to be with our partner in silence for short periods of time—without even being mad. But have you and your partner ever made a conscious decision to be together in silence for a longer period of time? Like for an hour or two or half a day? If you haven't, I highly recommend it because deciding to be together in the silence for a while can be one of the most intimate and rewarding things you can do with your partner.

You can decide to spend some time in silence together in the same way that you might decide to have sex or go for a walk or cook dinner together. When you decide, you can also decide on the duration—half an hour, an hour, two hours, an afternoon. Then you can sit silently and do nothing. Or you can meditate together. Or go for a walk in the woods or on the beach… in silence. Or go to town and walk around, hand in hand, without saying a word. You can try cooking dinner together and eating without words being spoken. Yes, the opportunities are truly endless. As a matter of fact, you can do most of the things you normally do together without saying anything!

Of course, part of the trick is not just to refrain from talking out loud but also to try to refrain from talking so much in your head. That, of course, is easier said than done! When you and your partner decide to try being together in the silence, you will probably discover in the beginning that it feels as if your thoughts are running totally wild inside your head. It's as if you are having even more thoughts than usual. Zoom, zoom, zoom. It's like being bombarded from all sides by thoughts crashing like a swarm of meteors into the earth's atmosphere. But in reality you don't have more thoughts than usual. It's just when you are silent, you really become aware of just how many thoughts you are having all the time. It can be amazing and quite shocking. If you're quiet enough for long enough, you'll even see the 101 myths about relationships arising in your head, trying like mad to drive you crazy!

One of the things that can help you reduce the amount of "talk" going on in your head when you are silent is to pay more attention to what is going on right now. If you can pay attention to what is happening right now, things will calm down. So if, for example, you are walking together in nature in silence, then notice the sounds, the smells, and everything you see. Feel the sensation of the earth under your feet. Listen to the sound of your footsteps. Notice the air flowing in and out of your body. Notice the silence between, behind and around the sounds. Notice this moment. Now. If you're having dinner together in silence, again notice the silence, this moment, what is happening right now, the food you are eating, the textures, the colors, the vegetables, the meal the two of you prepared together with love.

So yes, being with your partner in the silence can be one of the most intimate things you can do with another human being—to be there, to stand there, completely naked without any words. For it is in the silence, in the presence that we are beyond thoughts and words, that our true self is to be found.

Three ways to cultivate
love in your life
(and in your relationship)

Everyone's always talking about *love!* We're all seeking love and we all use enormous amounts of time and energy trying to "get" and experience love. Love, love—and more love.

But what is *love?* What is this thing called love which we are all seeking day and night—and which we seek most of all in our relationships? And how can we experience the love that we seek?

As I've been saying in this book, in reality, love is not something outside us. Love is something that's inside us because love is what we are—love is our nature—the nature of everything. As I also write, the only thing that is preventing us from experiencing our true love nature are the many thoughts and beliefs we have that have absolutely nothing to do with reality—thoughts that contradict the nature of love. On the previous pages of this book, I have tried to describe how you can identify and investigate these limiting thoughts and beliefs.

So what happens when you question your limiting thoughts and stories? What happens when you question all your "shoulds" and "shouldn'ts"? Especially when it comes to your relationship and your partner? When you do this, you actually experience *much more love.* You experience the love that has been there all the time, the love which is your true nature—but which has been clouded or veiled by your own confused thinking.

What you focus your attention on grows

In addition to questioning the thoughts that are preventing you from experiencing love, there is another approach you can use to experience more love in your life and in your relationship. This approach or technique—which I call *cultivating love*—is based on understanding a fundamental observation of the nature of mind, which I describe in the Introduction.

There is a cause-and-effect relationship between your thinking and your experience. Thought is cause, experience is effect.

Another way of formulating this observation is to say that *what you focus your attention on grows.* In practice this means that if you want to experience something in life, then it's a good idea to focus your attention on it. Because what you focus your attention on grows.

If you want to be more fully present in the now and not always so absorbed in the past or the future, then it's a good idea to focus on what is happening right now, right this moment wherever you are, sitting with this book in your hand, in this chair, with the floor underneath your feet and the air flowing in and out of your lungs… and not on your plans or your worries about the future.

If you want to experience more wealth in your life, it is a good idea to focus on all the wealth and support you already have in your life right now — on all the food in your refrigerator, all the clothes in your closet, all the good friends you have, all the sunshine, the beautiful starry sky, the rain and the trees… because what you focus your attention on grows.

The same holds true for love. If you want to experience more love in your life and in your relationship, it's a good idea to focus your attention on love. To dwell on the idea of love and to let your thoughts, words and actions express love. Because what you focus your attention on grows!

Cultivating love

So how do you focus on love in practice? How do you cultivate more love in your thinking and in your life? And not least, how do you cultivate more love in your relationship? On the following pages, I describe three good ways to focus on love and experience more love — and I call this *cultivating love.*

1) *Cultivating spaciousness*
2) *Cultivating support*
3) *Cultivating understanding*

Love is greater than a relationship

When you read about the three ways to cultivate love that I suggest, your first reaction might be — well what do these things have to do with being a couple?

The answer is they have absolutely nothing and absolutely everything to do with being a couple! They have nothing to do with couple relationships because love is something far greater and far more all-encompassing than the passing form of a relationship. Because love is our nature, love is everything, love is reality, love is you and me and everything that lives and breathes—love is every form, every relationship, every grain of sand, every galaxy in all of eternity. Love is God. The temporary joining together of two human beings in what we call a relationship is just one of love's many infinite manifestations.

At the same time, these techniques have everything to do with couple relationships because love includes everything and everyone, and includes every relationship. So the more we focus on and dwell on the nature of love, the more we experience love in all areas of our lives—including in our couple relationships (and also in your single life if you happen to be single).

True love has no boundaries

As you begin to regularly cultivate love in your life as described on the following pages, you will begin to experience more love in *all your relationships,* including your relationship with your partner—and not least in your relationship with yourself. This is because it's not possible to cultivate love in your relationship with your partner without it influencing your relationships with all the other people in your life. Nor is it possible to cultivate more love towards other people without it influencing the love you feel in your relationship with your partner. For true love—real, genuine, authentic love—is unconditional and unlimited. Real genuine love has nothing to do with the 101 myths about love and relationships either. Real love has no "shoulds" or "shouldn'ts". Real love has no expectations, no demands and no limits.

Here are my three ways to cultivate more love:

1. CULTIVATING SPACIOUSNESS

To cultivate a greater experience of love in your life, it is a good idea to cultivate spaciousness. Why? Because the reality is that life itself is spacious and has room enough for everything. Life or reality contains and allows everything. There is room enough for everything and everyone in life. Regardless of whom you are or how you feel, life embraces you. Life does not reject anyone. It doesn't matter if you are a man or a woman, if you're young or old, fat or thin, rich or poor, sick or healthy, beautiful or ugly, trendy or behind the times, famous or unknown—there is room for you in life because life embraces everyone and everything. It doesn't matter if you are confused or clear, conscious or unconscious, happy or unhappy—there is room enough for every thought and feeling no matter what it is. Life embraces and accepts everything. Life never suddenly says, "Hey you over there, you're not allowed to think or feel like you do. You're not allowed to weigh so much! You're not allowed to look like you look. You're not allowed to feel bad. No, no, no! Shame on you!" No, life never does that — ever. Life has room enough for everyone and everything. There are no limits to how much life can contain. Life contains both the sinner and the saint — the confused and the enlightened. Life is unlimited and unconditional acceptance, unlimited and unconditional love.

One of the reasons why we human beings don't experience the love that we seek is that our "love" is usually not as spacious or unconditional as life's. We usually say to our partners, our families, our friends and even to ourselves: "I will only love you if…" "I will only love you if you do what I want you to do." "I will only love you if you agree with me." "I will only love you if you live up to my expectations and ideas." "I will only love you if…" and so on. This conditional "love" (which isn't really love at all) closes us down so that we do not experience real love in our lives. When our minds close, our hearts close too. That is why one of the ways to cultivate love in your life is to cultivate spaciousness.

Cultivating spaciousness towards your partner

How would you feel if you were just as spacious and accepting towards your partner as life is? How would you feel if you could see, really see, that your partner is just the way he or she is right now? That your partner does what he does, says what he says, and is precisely the way he is whether you think he should be like that or not. How would you feel if you could see, really see, that your partner understands or doesn't understand just exactly what he or she understands right now — and not one bit more or less? How would you feel if you realized that your partner is interested in or not interested in exactly what he or she is interested in? How would you feel if you couldn't believe that your partner "should" be different than he or she is right now? What would happen if you just completely stopped trying to change your partner?

Cultivating spaciousness towards yourself

What about being more spacious and accepting towards yourself? How would you feel if you were just as spacious and accepting towards yourself as life is? If you could see, really see, that you are exactly the way you are right now — and it's OK? If you could see that yes, you think what you think, feel what you feel, and want or don't want what you want. If you really could see that this is how you are, right now. How would you feel if you couldn't believe the thought that you "should" be different and feel differently than you do right now — if you were just as spacious and accepting towards yourself as life is?

Wouldn't that feel, nice? Loving? Wouldn't it feel as if your heart was opening more and more… Wouldn't you feel rather spacious — both towards yourself and towards your partner?

When you do this and you feel it, you will begin to understand why I say that spaciousness is one of the ways to experience more love in your life. Because life is spacious. Because love is spacious. You are too when your thinking and your focus are in harmony with reality — in harmony with the way things really are.

A warning: Love misunderstood

When you start to really notice that life contains your partner exactly as he or she is at the moment and you begin to accept that your partner is the way he or she is, does this mean that you can't be assertive and set limits and say no to your partner? Does this mean that you always have to do what your partner asks? Does this mean that you can't ask your partner for what you want or suggest other ways of doing things?

No, absolutely not! And why should it? If you take a closer look, you will see that such thoughts are an absurd misunderstanding of the nature of love and spaciousness. When you think about it, what do these two things — the spacious nature of love and your saying yes or no — have to do with each other? Remember love embraces everything, including your yes and your no! Love includes everything you agree to as well as everything you don't agree to. Love includes both what you want and what your partner wants. Both the things you agree on and the things you don't agree on, your opinion and your partner's. Love / life has room enough for both of you whether you stay together or go your separate ways!

So please beware! Make sure that as you cultivate spaciousness towards your partner, it doesn't become what I call "love misunderstood". Make sure you don't mistakenly believe that spaciousness means you should become a "doormat" and not set limits or say no or take good care of yourself. Not setting limits has nothing whatsoever to do with love and spaciousness! Look at it this way, if you don't take good care of yourself, if you don't set limits and say no and do what feels right for you, is that love? Love for whom?

Who knows, maybe a no to your partner is also the best thing that can happen to your partner, even if your partner doesn't see it like this. Your no might be a sign that there's something better waiting for your partner out there (even if your partner doesn't believe it). Who knows, perhaps your partner can ask someone else, someone who is more able to give your partner what her or she wants than you are. Or maybe your partner can figure out how to give himself/herself whatever it is he or she wants.

If your partner is unhappy because you say no thanks to something, well, then you can also practice being spacious and accepting about the fact that your partner is unhappy!

2. CULTIVATING SUPPORT

Another good way to feel and experience more love in your life is to notice how everything in life is supporting you. Notice that the nature of life is to support everything. Always and without exception. Unconditional support.

Try to notice all the things that are supporting you right now, right this moment while you are sitting here, reading this book. The chair you are sitting in or the bed you are lying on are supporting you. The floor and the ground beneath your feet are supporting you. Gravity, the earth that holds you to its breast and makes sure you don't just float away into space, is supporting you. The air around you and in you is supporting you. The clothes on your body are supporting you and keeping you warm. Your body is supporting you all the time: the air that is streaming in and out of your lungs, all by itself, whether you notice it or not; your heart that is beating and pumping blood around in your veins; the skin that is keeping your body together. Your body is supporting you all the time: the air that is streaming in and out of your lungs, all by itself, whether you notice it or not; your heart that is beating and pumping blood around in your veins; the skin that is keeping your body together. Yes, everything is supporting you. If you really think about it, you won't be able to find anything in life which you can say for sure is not supporting you in one way or another. Because the nature of life is that it supports everything and everyone. This support is love.

It's not just the many different things in your life that are supporting you, it's also the many different people in your life who are supporting you and contributing to your life in one way or another. Think about it for a moment—the cashier at the supermarket who rings up your purchases so you can eat breakfast, lunch and dinner; the postman who delivers your letters and packages. The hairdresser who cuts your hair. The dentist who takes care of your teeth. The construction workers who helped build the house or building you live in. Your colleagues at work who support you in doing as good a job as you possibly can so you can also support other people with what you are doing! And what about your mother and father and your family and friends who are all supporting you and wishing you the very best in life (even if they sometimes have completely different ideas about what is best for you!). So think about it, and when you do, I am quite certain you won't be able to find a single person who you can say with absolute certainty isn't supporting you or contributing to your life in one way or the other.

So this is a good exercise if you want to experience more love in your life. I highly recommend you regularly use 5-10 minutes and just sit with your eyes closed and notice all the things in life that are supporting you right now—just as I described above. This is a wonderful meditation, which can really open your heart and your mind to all the love that is in you and around you all the time!

Your nature is also support

If you take time to notice, you will also discover that your nature is also to support everything else in life as well. That's what you are here for. If you are a baker, then you are supporting the rest of life by baking bread and rolls and cakes for other people. If you work in a bank then you are supporting life by managing people's money for them. If you are a parent, then you are supporting your children by taking care of them and teaching them how to manage in life. When you pay your taxes, you are supporting your society and your country and all the other people who live in it. When you spend time with your friends you are supporting them with your presence and your friendship. So yes, your nature is to support everything here in life too. Now isn't that a wonderful thing to think about! Everything is love and you are love!

Serving your fellow men and women

Another good way to cultivate love in the form of support is to ask yourself regularly, "How can I serve?" "How can I best help my fellow human beings?" "How can I contribute to the Highest Good in this situation?" Then listen to the answers or impulses that arise and follow them. This is love in action. So be love in action.

When you do this exercise, you can ask how you can help in a general way —and you can also ask how you can help (and provide support) in specific situations and to specific individuals.

Giving

Giving is another good way to cultivate love in the form of support in your life. This is because the nature of life is to give. Just think of what life is giving you all the time without ever asking for anything in return. The sun that is warming your body, the air you are breathing, all the gifts of nature, the earth you are walking upon, the rain that is falling, everything that is giving of itself all the time without ever asking for anything in return.

163

So another good way to cultivate more love in your life is to give without asking for anything in return. This is a good exercise because as you've probably noticed, we often give and expect to get something in return. Of course this is not really giving, but rather a form of barter or exchange. So try instead to give regularly to others without expecting anything in return.

Even better, try once in a while to give something to someone or do something for someone without them discovering that you were the giver—again because we usually hope that when we give something to someone, they will realize it was us and at least recognize our gift and maybe even tell us how good we are!

So try giving—it never fails to make you (and other people) happy!

Give what you want to receive

A good way to cultivate more support in your relationship is to focus on giving your partner whatever it is you would like to have your partner give you! If, for example, you want your partner to pay more attention to you, well then pay more attention to your partner! Ask your partner what he wants and then give it to him (also if he just wants to be left alone!). Be the partner you are seeking. Give what you want to receive in your relationship.

You can also cultivate support for yourself in your own life by giving yourself whatever it is you really want your partner to give you! If, for example, you want your partner to pay more attention to you—well then you do it! You give yourself more attention. You don't really need to wait for your partner to give you what you want because you can just do it yourself. If you are going to wait for your partner to give you something, you might have to wait forever! But you—you can do it right now. You can give yourself the attention you want, right now and every single minute of your life. You can work on understanding and appreciating and enjoying yourself more, right now. This, in fact, is your job. Nobody else can do it for you. Nobody else can take it from you. Which is pretty good news. You can do it for yourself! So why wait for your partner? (This doesn't mean you can't ask your partner for what you want. But after you have asked, there's nothing more you can do in terms of your partner. What your partner gives or doesn't give you is your partner's business and is out of your control.)

So regardless of what happens, the best thing you can do is be the partner you are dreaming of—both towards your partner and towards yourself. Give what you want to receive.

3) CULTIVATING UNDERSTANDING

A third way to cultivate love in your life is to cultivate understanding.

Why understanding?

Because we human beings often close our minds and our hearts to the things and people we don't understand. We often have a hard time embracing or accepting what we don't understand. In the old days when I didn't understand the reason for my suffering—which was my own innocent, confused thinking—I often just shut myself down. I condemned and rejected myself and then I condemned and rejected others. Which certainly wasn't love or spaciousness.

Now as my understanding grows, I can see that the more I understand my own innocently confused thinking and the suffering it causes, the more I am able to accept and feel compassion for myself and for others. This is love.

Understanding leads to love

When we understand how things are interconnected, our minds and hearts open and love flows freely. When we understand that we are all basically alike, love flows more freely. When we understand that we all are seeking the same thing—a happy life without suffering—love flows more freely. When we understand that we all suffer for the same reason (when our thinking is out of harmony with reality), love flows more freely. Finally, when we understand that none of us wishes to hurt ourselves or other people but that because of our innocence and ignorance, we do, then we can truly feel love and compassion for each other.

The "anatomy of a human being"

I call this understanding—understanding "the anatomy of the human being". It's a powerful way of cultivating love in your life. Why? Because this understanding brings greater spaciousness, compassion and love—towards oneself and other people. When you really see that you are just an innocent, confused child who is always trying the best you can, how can you reject or condemn yourself? When you see that everyone else is also just an innocent, confused child trying to do the best he or she can, how can you reject or condemn anyone?

Open mind, open heart

People often say it's important to have an open heart. But as long as your mind and your thinking are closed, how can you have an open heart? As long as you don't understand yourself or others or understand the anatomy of a human being, how can you have an open heart? It's just not possible. Because the mind (your thinking) is cause and your experience (whether your heart is open or closed) is the effect, in other words, the result of your thinking.

So a closed mind = closed heart.
An open mind = open heart.

It's as simple as that.

One of the best ways you can open your mind and your heart is to work on understanding how we human beings get to be the way we are. Nothing is more important than this!

To help you open your mind and heart, I have developed a meditation which I call "The Heathrow Airport Meditation". Try it when you're out traveling or when you're in a large group of people.

Heathrow Airport Meditation

Many years ago I was sitting in one of Heathrow Airport's many departure terminals waiting for my plane, which was delayed several hours. As you probably know, Heathrow Airport in London is one of the world's biggest and busiest airports, with tens of thousands of travelers passing through each and every day. The day my plane was delayed was no exception. In the terminal where I was sitting, hundreds and thousands of people were constantly passing by. Men and women, old and young, children and adults, from Europe, Asia, America, Africa—you name it. Watching the hordes of people passing by was like experiencing a mini cosmos of all of humanity. There were Indian men with turbans and full beards with their wives in long, colorful saris. There were dark-haired Italians wearing designer jeans and American tourists in Bermuda shorts. There were Japanese tourists with cameras around their necks and Danish business people talking on their cell phones. Everyone was there. All coming from somewhere; all going somewhere else. At some point in time, each and every one of these people would probably eat something, use the restroom, sit down somewhere or shop at some of the stores in this huge terminal while they waited for their flights to depart.

To pass the time I decided to play a little game with myself. The game was quite simple. I decided to try to answer the question: "What do I have in common with every human being—without exception—here at Heathrow Airport?" Then I tried to see how many things I could find that I had in common with all the other travelers in the airport.

It was an interesting exercise.

Here are some of the many things I discovered I had in common with all the travelers (and indeed every single human being on the planet):

We all live on the same beautiful Planet Earth and we're all breathing the same air. We're all walking on the same earth, under the same sun, with wind and oceans and rain and plants and animals. We're all a part of this thing called life...each and every one of us.

We're all basically seeking the same thing—a happy life without suffering. None of us wants to suffer. We all want to be happy, each and every one of us, without exception. We may have different ideas and beliefs about what it takes to be happy, but the basic impulse in the back of everything we do is always the same longing to be happy.

We all have a physical body that is either standing, sitting or lying down. A physical body that eats, drinks, goes to the toilet. A physical body that can get hot or cold, feel sick or weak. A body that was once very tiny and had to be cared for by its mother. A body that with the passing of time will age, get old and finally die and return to the earth...sooner or later. No matter how beautiful or strong or healthy our body is now, none of us will stay attached to the same body forever.

We all need food and water, a place to sleep and live, clothing and other basic material possessions. And we all have to somehow work for or contribute to getting these things, whether as a farmer, an account manager, shop clerk, politician, school teacher, doctor. We are all a part of the interconnectedness of humanity, the complex web of life.

We all have a mother and father, who also has a mother and father. We all have family and friends. We are all constantly relating to other people and we all have to somehow deal with this world—talk and communicate with each other, agree or disagree, say yes or no.

We all have thoughts and stories that constantly arise and disappear again like waves on the ocean, like rays from the sun, and when we believe these thoughts, we experience them. We all get to experience what we think, whether what we are thinking is true or not.

We all suffer for the same basic reason...because we believe in thoughts or have beliefs that have nothing to do with reality. And we all have had the experience of feeling afraid, lonely, anxious, angry, sad. And we've all experienced heartbreak.

We are all here now, which must mean that we all have the same equal right to be here...that we all have the same equal worth in the eyes of God or life...right now.

Yes, we all have so much in common—so much that there can be no doubt that we are all one big family of brothers and sisters.

As I gradually went through and meditated on the many things that I had in common with all the other travelers in the airport (and indeed every human being on the planet), I felt my mind opening. As my mind opened to our common humanity, our common nature, I felt my heart opening too. And I felt a great sense of love. Love for myself and for all the people that were passing through the airport. I felt this great sense of oneness, of belonging, a feeling that each and every one of these people, despite their varying physical disguises, really were my dear brothers and sisters! We really were one big family! Oh how my heart opened and expanded! My heart. Big heart! I felt as if all of Heathrow Airport and the whole world and all of life were just one big, soft, loving, beating heart, and there I was, sitting right in the heart of it! Flowing down the river of love with all the other drops of love. Yes, there was nothing but love. Love here, love there, love everywhere. Even now as I write this so many years later, I can still feel how I felt at that moment. It was an incredible feeling—a feeling of being home, of being OK, of being safe, of belonging.

After my first spontaneous "Heathrow Airport Meditation" that day, I have often used this meditation when I am with large groups of people—not only at airports, but if I'm at a concert, giving a lecture, or walking down some busy city High Street. Sometimes I even do this meditation when I'm all alone, just thinking about some group of people I am going to spend time with. Each time I do it, I feel the same heart opening and the same very special sense of love.

But don't believe me, try it for yourself—and feel the love!

Ten observations about the nature of relationships

Here are ten observations about the nature of relationships (and about human relationships in general) that can make your journey along the path of love a bit easier, a bit more joyful and a bit more loving. When you read these observations and contemplate them, please remember they don't have anything to do with "right" or "wrong", "good" or "bad", or "should" or "shouldn't". These observations are simply a description of the way things are, just like the law of gravity is a description of the ways things are.

Here are the ten observations:

OBSERVATION NO. 1:
You can't make me happy (that's my job)

Most of us have been brought up to believe that the way we feel—whether we're happy or unhappy—has something to do with the outer circumstances in our life. That the way we feel has something to do with our job, finances, health —or with our partner and relationship. At first glance, it may seem that this is the way things hang together. Because when something happens in the outer world, for example when our partner says or does something, we usually also do react and feel something. Maybe we feel good or maybe we feel discomfort, maybe we feel happy or maybe we feel sad. So this might seem to indicate that what our partner says or does is the reason for the way we feel and react.

But it this really true? Is it really true that what our partner says or does is the cause of our reaction?

Let's take an example. Let's say your boyfriend promised to call you this evening and he doesn't. How does this make you feel? How do you react? Are you sad? Worried? Angry? Or are you relieved because you had other plans? If this happens to ten different women, will they all react the same way as you? No, obviously not.

So the fact that people react differently to the exact same event shows us that the cause of our reaction cannot be in the event itself. Because if it was—if the event itself was the cause of our reaction — then every human being would react in the exact same way to the same event. But the reality is people don't. This shows us that there must be another cause or reason for the way we react. Since this cause is not in the event itself, the cause must be somewhere else — namely in our minds. The cause must be in the way we think or you could say in the way each of us individually interprets what's going on.

When you understand this and the cause-and-effect relationship between your thinking and your reaction, you will also understand why I can say that your partner cannot make you happy or unhappy. This is because the real cause of why you feel the way you feel — the real reason why you're happy or unhappy — is to be found in your interpretations of things, in other words in your thinking. This mechanism is equally true for everyone, including your partner.

For more about this observation, see the chapter "The only thing you can experience in your relationship is your own thinking" on page 72.

OBSERVATION NO. 2:
You can't make me unhappy (that's also my job)
Since my partner can't make me happy because the cause lies in my own thinking, it also means my partner can't make me unhappy either. Only my thinking can do this since my thinking determines how I feel.

What a relief to find out that my partner is not responsible for the way I feel or for what I'm thinking. (The reverse is also true: I'm not responsible for the way my partner feels either!)

This observation doesn't mean that we can't talk things over with our partners and be as kind, respectful and supportive of each other as we can. This observation is simply based on the fact that in the final analysis, the responsibility for the way I feel is to be found in my own thinking and in my own interpretation of events and of what my partners does or doesn't do.

So you can't make me unhappy. And I can't make you unhappy.

What a relief!

OBSERVATION NO. 3:
You can't give me anything I don't already have
This observation is the most important of the ten observations about the nature of relationships, and it says: Each one of us is already whole and complete in and of ourselves. Each one of us already is all the love and happiness we are seeking. This is so important to understand because when we see this and

understand that love is our true nature, so many of the collective myths about relationships and love simply crumble.

Unfortunately, when you believe our collective relationship myths, which say you are lacking something that only another person can give you, then it becomes very difficult to be a human being (in general) and to be in a relationship (in particular). The belief that another person can give you what you lack makes you a victim in your own life and leads to insecurity, neediness and low self-esteem. With this comes jealousy, possessiveness, control, manipulation and many of the behavioral traits that can really ruin a relationship for both you and your partner. Because regardless of how much attention, time and energy your partner gives you, you'll never really be satisfied because the basic problem is not what your partner does or doesn't do but your own insecurity and neediness.

When, however, you are conscious of the fact that both you and your partner are already whole and complete all by yourselves, then a relationship is no longer about two half people who are desperately trying to fill up the painful emptiness inside each other but rather about two whole human beings who are enjoying themselves together on the path of love.

OBSERVATION NO. 4:
You can't save me from my life
This observation is based on the realization that in the final analysis, each of us has to deal with life and everything that happens to us on our own. Each and every one of us must figure out what to do with our lives. Each and every one of us must discover how to deal with the issues of money, work, career, family, home and the world. This is something our partners can't do or fix for us — nor can our relationship. (This doesn't mean we can't help and support each other in life and on the path of love.)

But if you try to use your relationship to save you from your life, you're bound for trouble. If you try to use your relationship to avoid facing challenges in life because you have stressful thoughts about your own ability to manage in life, well then again you're heading for trouble. Quite simply, no relationship can do this for you. No relationship can save you from yourself.

For more about this observation, see the chapter "Are you in a relationship that's not good for you?" on page 91.

OBSERVATION NO. 5:
We have no future together (only this moment)
This observation is based on the recognition that a relationship — just like every-

171

thing else in life—is something that is happening now, in the present moment. The past is a thought you are having—now, in the present moment. The future is a thought you are having—now, in the present moment. The only thing you ever have is now.

This means if you use a lot of your mental energy thinking about the future, you miss the only thing you ever really have, which is now, the present moment. If you are always thinking about what you are going to do in the future as a couple or about what a relationship will lead to in the future, you are again missing the only thing two people really can have together, which is this moment. Two people who are walking, talking, touching, being together, making love—right now.

This doesn't mean you can't make plans for the future together. It just means it becomes problematic when we focus so much on the future and on where a relationship is going that we miss the wonder of the present moment and end up living as if the now is only a stepping stone on the way to some future goal. Because then what happens? After all your stress and strain and hard work—when you finally have the perfect two and a half kids, the perfect dream house, the perfect pension plan, the perfect designer kitchen and it's time to lean back and enjoy life—the idiot comes home and asks for a divorce because he's fallen in love with a younger woman.

So it's a good idea to keep mainly focused on whatever the two of you have going for you right now, in this moment. Because in fact, it's the only thing you actually do have. And the interesting thing is that when you begin to notice this, you may be pleasantly surprised to find out how much this really is, right here, right now.

And wasn't that why you wanted to be in a relationship in the first place—because you want to be happy? So remember to ask yourself—when is the only time you can actually be happy? Isn't it right now? Isn't it impossible to be happy somewhere out in the future?

Now is the only time you can ever be happy in your relationship.

So if not now, then when?

OBSERVATION NO. 6:
You can't promise me anything except that you can't promise me anything
This observation points to the fact that even though we as a couple have promised ourselves so many things, such as we'll be together until death do us part, the reality is that neither of us knows what tomorrow will bring. Or if we'll be able to keep our promises!

So why promise something or anything if you don't know for sure if you can keep your promise? Why, for example, promise you won't ever change when the reality is that people and things and relationships *do* change … sooner or later.

For more about this observation, see the chapter "Who needs 'commitment' when you have reality?" on page 84.

This also means…

OBSERVATION NO. 7:
You'll be faithful to me until you're not faithful anymore
Pretty obvious when you think about it. Just look at the divorce statistics!

OBSERVATION NO. 8:
No matter what I want you to do, you'll do exactly what you do anyway
With this observation, I don't mean you can't ask your partner for what you want. In fact, it's very important to learn to ask your partner for what you want. Remember your partner isn't a mind reader (see the chapter "Your partner isn't a mind reader" on page 40 for more about this).

This observation is based on the simple fact that after you have asked your partner for what you want, your partner will do precisely what he or she is doing or not doing. What your partner does is completely out of your control. The only thing you have control over (besides what you do) is what you ask your partner for, and how you choose to react in relation to what your partner does or doesn't do. Because once you've made a request, your job is done. Then if your partner happens to refuse your request, well then again it's up to you to decide what to do in relation to this. So, your partner won't give you what you want. What will you do about it? Will you ask again later? Or will you ask someone else for what you want? Or will you try to give yourself whatever you want, by yourself? Or maybe — if it's very important for you to have a partner who gives you what you asked for — you'll find a new partner who will give you what you want. It's all up to you.

For more about this observation see the chapter "Who would your partner be if you got your way?" on page 80.

OBSERVATION NO. 9:
No matter how hard I try, you're never going to change (what I see is what I get)
The reality is you are exactly the way you are, right now. The reality is your partner is exactly the way he or she is, right now. But how many of us really base our relationships on this fact? Unfortunately, many of us base our relationships on the idea or hope that if we work hard enough on our partner, he or she will

eventually change! But how often does this happen? How often do our partners actually change and become the people we want them to be?

So who would you be in your relationship right now if you based your behavior on how your partner really is (and I mean really is) right NOW—and not on some hope for a change for the better? Who would you be if you simply couldn't believe that your partner would ever change? If you knew that what you see right now is all you are ever going to get??? Now and forever? For many people, realizing this can be quite an eye-opener. I call it a reality check!

(Some years ago, I did a workshop in Sweden with Barbara Berger with more than a hundred women attending. We did an exercise where all the participants were asked to explore how they would be in their relationships if they looked reality in the eye when it came to their partners and accepted the fact that their partners would never change. After the workshop, four of the women came up to us and told us they had decided to leave their husbands immediately! Several other women had the opposite reaction and told us about the positive changes they were going to make in their relationships now that they had actually looked at the reality of who their men really were instead of focusing on some hopelessly unrealistic expectations to their partners!)

This observation can also help us become more aware of another important thing when it comes to relationships—namely the only thing we can ever change is us! You can only change you! But you can't change your partner, no matter how hard you try!

What a relief to find this out!

For more about how to become more aware of the difference between reality and your expectations to your partner, see the chapter "Expectations & Reality" on page 144.

OBSERVATION NO. 10:
You love me—and that doesn't mean you'll do what I want
As I wrote in the chapter "Are women to blame for all the porn?" on page 31, one of the most painful relationship myths is the myth that "if you love me, you'll do what I want". If you look closely, you'll see that this myth has nothing to do with reality when it comes to relationships. If you look closely you'll see that yes, people in relationships do love each other. But does this mean they always want the same thing? Or are always in agreement? Absolutely not! So the belief in this myth can really lead to a lot of confusion and unhappiness in relationships.

Ten observations about the nature of relationships (the short version)

1. You can't make me happy (that's my job).

2. You can't make me unhappy (that's also my job).

3. You can't give me anything I don't already have.

4. You can't save me from my life.

5. We have no future together (only this moment).

6. You can't promise me anything except that you can't promise me anything.

7. You'll be faithful to me until you're not faithful anymore.

8. No matter what I want you to do — you'll do exactly what you do anyway.

9. No matter how hard I try, you're never going to change (what I see is what I get).

10. You love me — and that doesn't mean you'll do what I want.

Epilog: Before and after

Before this book

- You're single and on your own and without a partner …
  and you hate it.

- You've met someone and you're not really sure where it's all going
  … and you hate it.

- You're sort of involved with someone and you're not really getting
  what you want … and you hate it.

- You've finally got the "whole package" complete with two and a
  half kids, the house, the dog and the retirement plan, and your
  whole life is pretty much planned till the day you die … and you
  hate it.

- You're on your way out of a relationship and you don't know what
  the future will bring … and you hate it.

- You're single and on your own and without a partner again …
  and you hate it!

After this book

- You're single and on your own and without a partner …
  and you love it.

- You've met someone and you're not really sure where it's all going
  … and you love it.

- You're sort of involved with someone and you're not really getting
  what you want … and you love it.

- You've finally got the "whole package" complete with two and a
  half kids, the house, the dog and the retirement plan, and your
  whole life is pretty much planned till the day you die … and you
  love it.

- You're on your way out of a relationship and you don't know what
  the future will bring … and you love it.

- You're single and on your own and without a partner again …
  and you love it!

The short version:
Overview of the exercises and
mythbusting techniques

Two good ways to say no (page 35)

If your partner is pressuring you to do what she (or he) wants by criticizing you, you can use:

Fogging (page 36)

Instead of defending yourself when you are criticized or entering into a long-winded discussion about the matter, you simply "fog" your partner. You answer by saying your partner might be right in his/her criticism ("You could be right") and that your answer is still no ("This weekend I'm planning on going fishing with my friends").

Negative inquiry (page 37)

Instead of defending yourself when you are criticized, you ask for further clarification of your partner's criticism ("I don't understand—is there something wrong with me going fishing with my friends this weekend?"). And you continue asking questions ("I don't understand? Why is this a problem? So what if it takes all day?") until your partner tells you what it is she/he really wants ("I want you go with me and visit my family this weekend"). You can then decide what you want to do about it. ("That sounds like a great idea, sweetheart, and I'm really glad you asked me. And this weekend my plan is to go fishing with my buddies. Maybe I can join you the next time you visit your family.")

Investigate why it's difficult to say no (page 39)

1) Write down on a piece of paper all the reasons why you have difficulty saying no to your partner.
2) Then investigate each reason with one of the mythbusting techniques described in Part Two of this book (page 137).

Asking your partner for what you want (page 40)

If you have difficulty asking your partner for what you want, practice by asking your partner for something at least three times a day. Ask directly, without any explanation or justification. Try to accept your partner's answer, whether it's a yes or a no, with open arms. Let your partner know that you love and accept him or her 100 percent, whether or not he/she says yes to your request.

Finding your core values (page 52)

Ask yourself these questions and answer as honestly as you can:

QUESTION: What is really important to me in a relationship?

ANSWER: For example, that my partner is honest with me and we are good at communicating.

QUESTION: What do I feel when my partner is honest with me and we are good at communicating?

ANSWER: I feel SAFE.

CONCLUSION: So feeling SAFE is one of your core values.

Ask yourself the questions until you have come up with three to five core values. When you are done, prioritize the values so you have a list that looks like this: *My core values when it comes to relationships are:*

1) Safety
2) Togetherness
3) Happiness

Identify your "Attachment Fetish Person" (page 53)

This fun and enlightening exercise will help you become more aware of the type of woman or man you're attracted to. Do as follows:

- Take a sheet of paper and divide it into three columns.
- In the left column write the names of the partners you've had in your life (including your present partner if you have one).
- In the middle column you write next to each partner's name a few words about his or her physical appearance.
- In the right column you write next to each partner's name a few words about his or her personality traits.
- Go through the middle and right column and see if some of the physical or personality traits appear several times. Check off the traits that appear more than once. These recurring physical and personality traits are probably the traits that characterize your "Attachment Fetish Person".

Cultivate the qualities
you are attracted to (page 55)

A good technique for getting more of the qualities you feel attracted to in your life is:

1) For each quality you are attracted to find at least three concrete examples of how you yourself have or express this quality in your life.

2) If you have difficulty finding a certain quality in yourself and would like to experience more of it, ask yourself what you can do to cultivate more of this quality in your life — and do it.

When you're stuck in a relationship
that's not good for you (page 91)

If you feel stuck in a relationship that's not good for you and you are having difficulty ending it, the following can help you:

1) **Look at the practical consequences** (page 91)
   If you are afraid of the practical consequences of ending the relationship, write down what you fear will happen if you break up — and then investigate these troubling thoughts with one of the mythbusting techniques described in Part Two of this book (page 137).

2) **Look at the beliefs** (page 93)
   If your beliefs are stopping you from ending the relationship, then write down these beliefs and investigate them with one of the mythbusting techniques described in Part Two (page 137).

3) **Look at Attachment Hunger** (page 94)
   If you're suffering from "Attachment Hunger":

- Remind yourself of the following: The powerful, at times almost overwhelming attraction and longing you feel to be together with the other person does not come from your soul or from your wisdom and sanity. It has its origin in an infantile longing to recreate the feeling of oneness, safety and love that you feel you lost in your early childhood. Let your choices and actions be governed by the wise, mature part of you — not by the infantile, immature part of you.

- Make a list of the negative, unhealthy and destructive consequences the relationship has for you and your life. Read your list when the longing to be with the other person is most intense and feels almost irresistible.

- Focus on experiencing oneness and love in other, more healthy ways. For example, by spending time in nature, helping others, doing service, focusing on the oneness and love you experience with your family and friends, playing with the kids, giving lots of loving hugs. You can also paint, sing, dance, write or express yourself creatively. Or spend time on personal development, spiritual practice or going to therapy.

Be the partner you seek (page 98)

1) Make a list of the things you want a partner or your partner to be and do for you. For example: "I want my partner to be better at telling me how he really feels."
2) Turn the list around. For example: "I want me to be better at telling me how I really feel."
3) Ask yourself how good you are at giving yourself each of the items on your list.
4) If you discover that there are things on your list that you are not that good at giving yourself, then ask yourself what you can do to give yourself what you want — and do it.
Give yourself what you want a partner or your partner to give you.

Cultivate your "relationship" with yourself (page 100)

A good way to cultivate your "relationship" with yourself is to regularly spend some time on your own in silence. Just you being together with you. Just sit in a chair and stare into space. In the silence. In this moment. Who are you? What are you thinking? What do you feel? How are you doing? Take the time to really notice.

"Do-nothing-meditation" (page 102)

We're often so busy doing and achieving that we don't notice that we already have everything we need to be happy, right here, right now. A good way to become more conscious of this is to sit still and do nothing for a while:
- Don't do anything—no reading or eating or listening to music.
  Just sit with your eyes open and look straight ahead.
- Don't speak.
- Don't get involved with the thoughts that arise and disappear in your mind. Each time you become aware that you have now become involved in one of the thoughts, have followed one of the thoughts, just stop and return to sitting and observing and doing nothing.
- Don't "meditate" (in the traditional sense of the word) or do any kind of "consciousness work". Just leave the mind completely alone and let it do what it does.

184

- If a stressful thought keeps arising and you can see that you are attached to it you can investigate the thought. For example, if you think "This is a complete waste of time" or "I have so much to do", then investigate each thought silently in your head with the four questions of The Work (page 149).
- Then return to just sitting and doing nothing.

Where does the love come from? (page 116)

A good exercise to become more aware of where the love and happiness you experience—for example, when you are with your partner—really comes from, is:
- Remember a time in your life when you experienced love. Notice how this feels.
- Ask yourself where these feelings come from?
- Write down a few words that describe what the feeling of love is for you.
- For each word or feeling, find at least three specific examples of how you yourself have or express or experience this feeling in your life.
- Notice all the love there is in your life now—with or without a partner.

Mythbusting (page 141)

1. Understand that your thinking is the reason why you feel like you do.
2. Notice what you are thinking when you feel upset.
3. Notice the difference between the thought and reality.
4. Notice how you feel when you stick to reality.
5. Make regular reality checks.

Expectations & Reality (page 144)

To see the difference between you expectations (for example, about your partner) and reality, examine the following:
1) **Expectations**
   Write down three things you think your partner should do (or not do) that would make your relationship better.
2) **Reality**
   What is the reality compared to the three things you have written on your list?
3) **Feelings**
   Notice how it feels to be realistic and see what the reality about your partner is in each of these three areas.

4) Action

Explore how you are going to act differently now that you see the reality about your partner.

The Work of Byron Katie (page 149)

Identify the thought, belief or story that is making you unhappy and write it down on a piece of paper. Then investigate the thought with the following four questions:

1. Is it true?
2. Can you absolutely know that it's true?
3. How do you react when you believe that thought?
4. Who would you be without the thought?
   Turn the thought around.

Being together in the silence (page 155)

One of the most intimate things you can do with your partner is to make a conscious decision to be together in silence for a while. You can sit quietly and do nothing or go for a walk in the woods. Notice the silence. Notice what is happening in this now moment.

Three ways to cultivate love in your life (and in your relationship) (page 157)

1) Cultivating spaciousness (page 159)

Notice that life contains everything and everyone, regardless of who you are or how you feel or what is going on.

- Cultivate spaciousness towards your partner: Notice that life contains your partner just the way he or she is right now, no matter what, regardless of how he or she is or isn't.
- Cultivate spaciousness towards yourself. Notice that life contains you just the way you are right now, no matter what, regardless of what you do or don't do.

2) Cultivating support (page 162)

Notice all the things that are supporting you:

- Sit in a comfortable position with your eyes closed and notice all the things that are supporting you, right now. The chair, the air, the floor, your breathing, gravity…
- You can also expand the meditation and reflect on how the many differ-

ent people in your life are supporting you. Your family, your friends, the postman, the cashier in the supermarket, the garbage collector, the nurse, society…
- You can also reflect on how you support your surroundings—with your work, your presence, your friendship, your support…

Serve your fellowmen and women:
- Ask yourself regularly, "How can I serve?" "How can I best help my fellow human beings?" "How can I contribute to the Highest Good in this situation?" Listen to the answers or impulses that arise and follow them. You can ask how you can help in a general way—and you can also ask how you can help (and provide support) in specific situations and with specific individuals.

Give:
- Give without asking for anything in return.
- Give to someone without them discovering that you were the giver.

Give what you want to receive in your relationship:
- Give your partner whatever you would like to have your partner give you: attention, support, acceptance and spaciousness, love…
- Give yourself whatever it is you really want your partner to give you: attention, support, acceptance and spaciousness, love…

3) Cultivating understanding (page 165)
Heathrow Airport Meditation (page 166)
- When you're with a large group of people, ask yourself: "What do I have in common with every human being in this place? What do I have in common with every man, woman and child—without any exceptions?" "What do I have in common with every human being on the planet?" See how many answers you can come up with, how many things we human beings have in common.

Recommended reading
about relationships
and relationship myths

BARBARA BERGER
Are You Happy Now? 10 Ways to Live a Happy Life
 A clear investigation of the difference between the goodness of reality and
 our thinking. Chock-full of good observations and tools for mythbusting—for example in romantic relationships and other close relationships.
The Awakening Human Being: A Guide to the Power Mind (with Tim Ray).
 The "Getting Real" textbook. Clear explanation of the mental laws and
 the way the mind works. Offers many practical techniques and conscious-
 ness-expanding exercises to improve one's life.

BYRON KATIE
Loving What Is: Four Questions That Can Change Your Life (Three Rivers
Press, 2003).
 The basic textbook of The Work. Groundbreaking guide. The direct path
 to freedom. A classic.
*I Need Your Love—Is That True?: How to Stop Seeking Love, Approval, and
Appreciation and Start Finding Them Instead* (Harmony Books, 2005).
 A guide to The Work with a focus on romantic relationships and other
 close relations. Another gem.
A Thousand Names for Joy: Living in Harmony with the Way Things Are
(Crown Archetype, 2007).
 A mind-boggling glimpse of how life and (relationships) are when you no
 longer believe your thinking. Destined to be a spiritual classic.

HARRIET B. BRAIKER
The Disease to Please: Curing the People-Pleasing Syndrome (McGraw-Hill,
2002).
 If you're a "people-pleaser", this book is for you. If you're afraid of conflict and anger or if you have problems saying no and setting limits

—this insightful and practical handbook (with a 21-day action plan) can really help.

HOWARD M. HALPERN
How to Break Your Addiction to a Person (Bantam, 2003).
If you're in a relationship that's not good for you and are having trouble breaking free, this book can help you understand why. If you believe that strong attraction equals a good match—Halpern's explanation of "Attachment Hunger" can be a real life-saver.

JANET SHIBLEY HYDE
The Gender Similarities Hypothesis
Can be downloaded for free on the Internet at
http://www.apa.org/journals/releases/amp606581.pdf
Groundbreaking study of the similarities and differences between men and women.

MANUEL J. SMITH
When I Say No, I Feel Guilty (Bantam, 1985).
The classic book about assertiveness. If you have problems setting limits and saying no to your partner, boss, children, mother-in-law or even the telephone salesman, this brilliant and practical book is a must.

MELODY BEATTIE
Codependent No More: How to Stop Controlling Others and Start Caring for Yourself (Hazelden, 1986).
Pioneering book about codependency. If you have a pattern of trying to "fix" people or save your partner, this book can be a lifesaver.
Beyond Codependency: And Getting Better All the Time (Hazelden, 1989).
More good stuff about codependency.

OSHO
From Sex to Superconsciousness (Full Circle Publishing, 2003).
Landmark book about the nature of sex, orgasm and love. A classic.

Visit www.beamteam.com
for more about Tim Ray

Books and CDs

Lectures and workshops

Private sessions

Bonus tracks

Newsletter

Web shop

FINDHORN PRESS

Life-Changing Books

For a complete catalogue,
please contact:

Findhorn Press Ltd
117-121 High Street,
Forres IV36 1AB,
Scotland, UK

t +44 (0)1309 690582
f +44 (0)131 777 2711
e info@findhornpress.com

or consult our catalogue online
(with secure order facility) on
www.findhornpress.com

For information on the Findhorn Foundation:
www.findhorn.org